NEW DIRECTIONS FOR ADULT AND CONTINUING EDUCATION

Ralph G. Brockett, *University of Tennessee, Knoxville*
EDITOR-IN-CHIEF

Alan B. Knox, *University of Wisconsin, Madison*
CONSULTING EDITOR

Experiential Learning: A New Approach

Lewis Jackson
University of Northern Colorado

Rosemary S. Caffarella
University of Northern Colorado

EDITORS

Number 62, Summer 1994

JOSSEY-BASS PUBLISHERS
San Francisco

EXPERIENTIAL LEARNING: A NEW APPROACH
Lewis Jackson, Rosemary S. Caffarella (eds.)
New Directions for Adult and Continuing Education, no. 62
Ralph G. Brockett, Editor-in-Chief
Alan B. Knox, Consulting Editor

Microfilm copies of issues and articles are available in 16mm and 35mm,
as well as microfiche in 105mm, through University Microfilms Inc., 300
North Zeeb Road, Ann Arbor, Michigan 48106-1346.

LC 85-644750   ISSN 0195-2242   ISBN 0-7879-9956-3

NEW DIRECTIONS FOR ADULT AND CONTINUING EDUCATION is part of The
Jossey-Bass Higher and Adult Education Series and is published quarterly
by Jossey-Bass Inc., Publishers, 350 Sansome Street, San Francisco,
California 94104-1342 (publication number USPS 493-930). Second-class
postage paid at San Francisco, California, and at additional mailing
offices. POSTMASTER: Send address changes to New Directions for Adult
and Continuing Education, Jossey-Bass Inc., Publishers, 350 Sansome
Street, San Francisco, California 94104-1342.

SUBSCRIPTIONS for 1994 cost $47.00 for individuals and $62.00 for institutions, agencies, and libraries.

EDITORIAL CORRESPONDENCE should be sent to the Editor-in-Chief, Ralph
G. Brockett, Department of Educational Leadership, University of
Tennessee, 239 Claxton Addition, Knoxville, Tennessee 37996-3400.

Cover photograph by Wernher Krutein/PHOTOVAULT © 1990.

Manufactured in the United States of America. Nearly all Jossey-Bass
books, jackets, and periodicals are printed on recycled paper that contains
at least 50 percent recycled waste, including 10 percent postconsumer
waste. Many of our materials are also printed with vegetable-based inks;
during the printing process, these inks emit fewer volatile organic com-
pounds (VOCs) than petroleum-based inks. VOCs contribute to the formation of smog.

Contents

Editors' Notes

Life can only be understood backwards; but it must be lived for-
wards.
                                                              —Kierkegaard

No man's knowledge here can go beyond his experience.
                                                              —John Locke

In his longitudinal examination of the adult lives of American citizens who were children during the great depression, the noted sociologist John Clausen (1993, pp. 16–17) commented, "Life is a series of transitions—transitions from one school to another, from dependency to economic self-support, from sin-glehood to marriage and family roles," from one job or career to another, from harboring prejudices to embracing diversity, and so on. Within a rapidly changing technological society such as ours, learning to prepare for, and cope with, transitions has become a lifelong enterprise for all citizens. Moreover, in contrast to earlier times, the directions that lives can take and the choices that adults need to make are considerably more numerous and complex. This has often meant that the assessment of new opportunities and ways of being, based on past and present experiences, has replaced tradition and ritual as the basis for making choices in the life-planning process.

Educators of adults who subscribe to the concepts and principles of experiential learning continue to be at the forefront of providing alternative frameworks and practical tools for assisting adults in defining and mapping out the choices that accompany life's transitions. In responding to the chal-lenge of helping adults give meaning to and make choices in the life planning process, institutions offering programs for adult learners often incorporate into their instructional activities ways for adults to actively use and reflect on their own experiences.

The purpose of this volume, *Experiential Learning: A New Approach,* is to provide a comprehensive model of experiential learning for instructors of adults in formal educational programs. There are two major messages we hope to convey through our discussions of the model. The first message is that link-ing the conceptual foundations of experiential learning to actual instructional applications is a key to effective practice. The second message is that paying attention to the assessment component of experiential learning is as impor-tant as the process of making choices about which methods and techniques should be selected to encourage learners to use and reflect on their own expe-rience. The model that is proposed in this volume evolved out of the work of an interdisciplinary study team at the University of Northern Colorado, the Experiential Learning Study Group. This group was formed in 1991 to explore the interrelationships between and among classroom instruction, field experiences (such as internships and practicums), and emerging developments in authentic and portfolio assessment. The focus of our initial work was on adult learners returning to postsecondary education. In this volume, as noted above, we have extended our application of the model to adult learners in all types of settings.

In Chapter One, Linda Lewis and Carol Williams review the origins and provide an overview of experiential learning. They then cite cutting-edge examples that illustrate how current applications integrate experiential learning into the practice of educating adults, using the settings of higher education and the workplace. In their discussions, Lewis and Williams reflect on the many different perspectives that have contributed to how experiential learning is conceptualized and on the increasing relevance of experiential learning models in the preparation of adult learners for the "unspecified challenges" of our rapidly changing society.

Lewis Jackson and Doug MacIsaac, in Chapter Two, provide an overview of the experiential learning model that is the centerpiece of this work. They first discuss four key issues that are especially relevant to the development of a contemporary model of experiential learning. The remainder of the chapter is devoted to introducing the five components of the experiential learning model, each of which is discussed in depth in subsequent chapters. A flowchart of the model is also presented in this chapter.

In Chapter Three, Rosemary Caffarella and Bruce Barnett highlight the first two components of the model, "Characteristics and Needs of Adult Learners" and "Conceptual Foundations of Experiential Learning." The combination of each of these theory and empirical knowledge bases form the conceptual foundation on which this model of experiential learning is grounded. Each of these broad bases is addressed using a thematic framework, giving brief descriptions of the salient work in adult and experiential learning.

Patty Lee and Rosemary Caffarella, in Chapter Four, present the third component of the model, "Methods and Techniques for Engaging Learners in Experiential Learning Activities." Three important guideposts for selecting and using experiential learning methods and techniques are first described. These authors then provide descriptions of specific instructional techniques for in-class and field-based learning activities and conclude with a discussion of how important it is to coordinate and balance in-class and field-based opportunities when designing learning programs for adults.

In Chapter Five, Bruce Barnett and Patty Lee present the fourth component of the model, "Assessment Processes and Outcomes: Building a Folio." The argument is made that folios are one way to ensure that "authentic" measures of what adults have learned through a variety of learning activities are collected over time. The two major types of materials that can be included in the folio—artifacts and attestations—are described, followed by suggestions for adult educators who assist learners in developing their folios.

Doug MacIsaac and Lewis Jackson, in Chapter Six, present the final component of the model, "Assessment Processes and Outcomes: Portfolio Construction." A working definition of a portfolio is first outlined, and the link is made between how to use the folio materials in the building of a portfolio. Emphasized in the chapter is how a portfolio's function should drive the process of selecting learning products for portfolio inclusion. The chapter concludes with a discussion of the importance of learner reflection with respect to the design and use of portfolios.

Diane Bassett and Lewis Jackson, in Chapter Seven, provide illustrations of how the model can be applied in a variety of higher education and workplace settings. They point out that, although the literature contains many discussions of exemplary applications of experiential learning and authentic assessment technology, applications that fully meet the specifications of the model are scarce in the literature. They review the model components, then offer specific examples of model applications in teacher education, educational technology, adventure programs, adult literacy, and diversity training.

The final chapter, by Lewis Jackson and Rosemary Caffarella, is designed to offer future directions for practice and research in experiential learning that are derived from the model. The four specific issues that are discussed are experiential learning in relation to human diversity, experiential learning and the social affiliation patterns of adults, experiential learning in relation to transfer of learning, and the emerging importance of authentic assessment. The last section reviews these issues and offers a final synthesis and reflection.

The experiential learning model that is described in these chapters offers a schema for the learning-to-assessment progression that we believe is a functional way of conceptualizing the contribution of experiential learning in the lives of lifelong learners. The model provides a framework for revisiting traditional assessment and instructional practices, for enhancing practices already designed from an experiential learning viewpoint, and for framing future inquiry into teaching and learning issues related to learning in adulthood.

We wish to thank Dorothy Hinojosa of the Center for Research on Teaching and Learning for her invaluable assistance in the preparation of this volume.

Finally, we would like to draw the reader's attention to the pattern of authorship found in this volume: It is one of multiple authors representing diverse fields of interest. This work, then, is truly a multidisciplinary effort. It is driven by the premise that scholarship is advanced when professionals representing both divergent and convergent perspectives collaborate in the discovery and dissemination of emergent knowledge. We hope that this work will contribute to the advancement of a multiple perspectives approach to experiential learning and to the education of adult learners.

Lewis Jackson
Rosemary S. Caffarella
Editors

Reference

Clausen, J. A. *American Lives: Looking Back at the Children of the Great Depression.* New York: Free Press, 1993.

LEWIS JACKSON *is associate professor in the Division of Special Education at the University of Northern Colorado.*

ROSEMARY S. CAFFARELLA *is professor in the Division of Educational Leadership and Policy Studies at the University of Northern Colorado.*

Methods and techniques that utilize learners' previous experiences, link conceptual foundations to practice, and encourage reflection are pivotal to the learning process.

Experiential Learning: Past and Present

Linda H. Lewis, Carol J. Williams

In its simplest form, experiential learning means learning from experience or learning by doing. Experiential education first immerses adult learners in an experience and then encourages reflection about the experience to develop new skills, new attitudes, or new ways of thinking.

During the last decade experiential learning has moved from the periphery of education to the center. No longer supplemental to the acquisition of content, experiential approaches are considered fundamental to meaningful learning. What accounts for this shift in perspective?

First, there has been a dramatic change in our conception of learning. We have moved away from behaviorist notions of teachers as purveyors of knowledge and learners as passive receivers. Current cognitive, humanistic, social, and constructivist learning models stress the importance of meaning formation. Therefore, models of good practice in adult education must utilize learners' previous experiences in order to enhance their current and future learning.

Second, in the last few decades, higher education has experienced an unprecedented influx of adult learners. Adult learners bring to the learning setting a wealth of prior experience and are eager to draw upon their background and previous learning in the classroom. Responsive teachers are able to capitalize on the prior experience of their students as a catalyst for new learning.

Third, in today's rapidly changing environment there is an increased demand for flexibility and the capacity to leverage previous knowledge and experience in new and different ways. Educators are being held accountable for what learners know and are able to do. The pressure for accountability has caused educators to design competency-based measures of learning and experiential techniques for assessing learner outcomes. The corporate sector, too, has called for greater accountability to justify the large sums of money spent on education and training, as it has been difficult to assess the transfer of training to the job. Experiential approaches appear to be more effective in developing skills that employers seek, such as communication skills, the ability to work in teams, and workplace literacy.

In this chapter, we begin by tracing the origins of experiential learning theory. We then move to an examination of theories that view experience as the key to meaningful learning and learning as the key to personal development. Giving special attention to higher education and workplace learning, we provide examples of current applications and conclude by examining the benefits and challenges of experiential approaches. Throughout this chapter, we demonstrate ways in which experiential learning theory provides a valuable framework for strengthening the critical linkages that can and must be developed among education, work, and personal development (Kolb and Lewis, 1986).

Historical Background

The experiential learning movement of the mid-nineteenth century represented an attempt in the United States to shift from formal, abstract education, where teachers present information and hope that students will later apply the knowledge, to more experience-based approaches. Laboratory sciences, applied studies, and clinical experiences were introduced on college campuses at that time. Early in the twentieth century, cooperative education, which referred to various kinds of off-campus experiences, was introduced as a complement to classroom instruction. During this time, John Dewey published *Experience and Education,* offering a justification for learning by doing.

Dewey stressed that the creation of new knowledge or the transformation of oneself through learning to perform new roles was more fundamental than simply learning how to do something. For him, experiential learning meant a cycle of "trying" and "undergoing" by becoming aware of a problem, getting an idea, trying out a response, experiencing the consequences, and either confirming or modifying previous conceptions. This process has the potential to result in a person's cognitive reconstruction of experience and significant personal learning such as overcoming one's biases. Such ongoing meaning-making over time leads to learning to learn experientially.

David Kolb's 1984 book on experiential learning is one of the more influential works linking theory to actual practice. Kolb proposes learning as the process whereby knowledge is created through the transformation of experience. In his model, true learning is depicted as a four-part process. Learners have *concrete experiences;* then they reflect on the experiences from a variety of perspectives. From these *reflective observations* learners engage in *abstract conceptualization,* creating generalizations or principles that integrate their observations into theories. Learners then use these generalizations as guides to engage in further action, called *active experimentation,* where they test what they have learned in other more complex situations. This in turn leads to another set of concrete experiences and another round of learning at a more sophisticated level. Kolb theorizes that learning increases in complexity through this process, and thus the learning cycle is transformed into a learning spiral of ever-increasing complexity.

Kolb posits two opposing ways of grasping or taking in information (concrete experience versus abstract conceptualization) and two opposing ways of transforming or processing that information (reflective observation versus active experimentation). The combination of preferred means of grasping and transforming information represents a learning style; however, Kolb considers any one learning style to be an incomplete form of processing information. For meaningful learning to occur, that is, learning that fully transforms one's understanding, all four stages of the cycle must be negotiated by the learner. To Kolb, an experience that is not reflected upon is unrealized learning.

Other writers interested in adult learning also stress the pivotal role of experience. Mezirow (1981, 1990) introduced the ideas of Habermas (1972), positing that emancipatory knowledge fosters critical reflection. Through critical reflection people become aware of the cultural and psychological assumptions that have influenced the way they see themselves and the way they structure their lives.

Freire (1970) as well believes the goal of education is to raise the critical consciousness of learners by means of experiential encounters with the realities of their culture. Both Freire and Mezirow believe in transformational learning. In Mezirow's view, transformational learning is directed toward personal development, while Freire conceives of transformational learning as social change. Feminist scholars have also added to the dialogue on emancipatory education, stressing that women's learning experiences should integrate subjective personal knowledge with objectively obtained knowledge in order to promote independent thinking (Tisdell, 1993).

Over the past fifty years, each of the aforementioned theorists and practitioners has made a significant contribution to our understanding and acceptance of experiential learning. From the foundation they have laid, new experiential approaches continue to evolve, enabling us to respond and adapt to dramatic and unanticipated changes. Now, with a greater commitment than ever before, both the public and private sectors are incorporating innovative experiential approaches to ensure relevance and to meet the needs of diverse groups.

Current Applications of Experiential Learning in Higher Education

There are three distinct applications of experiential learning in higher education: field-based experiences, prior learning assessment, and experiential applications for personal development and classroom-based learning. Each is described below.

Field-Based Experiential Learning in Higher Education. Field-based experiences, the oldest area of interest, have been common in higher education since the 1930s. Internships and practicum assignments help prepare students for careers in medicine, clinical psychology, education, and social work. Cooperative education, in which students alternate periods of full-time, off-campus employment with periods of full-time study, has been popular in the last several decades.

Another variation, service learning, in which students perform community service for others, is currently popular on college campuses. The concept expands upon the idea of volunteerism by including a reflective component, by emphasizing the transfer of learning between server and those served, and by encouraging students to view problems in a larger societal context. Service learning provides students with opportunities to analyze social problems, identify community resources, and take responsibility for helping to address societal problems.

Credit for Prior Learning. Credit for prior learning, a second major strand of interest in experiential learning, reflects the recognition by the higher education establishment that meaningful learning can and does occur in informal settings. Principles and procedures for evaluating prior learning at the undergraduate level have been evolving since the 1970s. The American Council on Education (ACE) has been a pioneer in developing credit recommendations for noncollegiate instruction such as in the military and more recently in large corporate training programs.

One widely recognized mechanism for evaluating prior learning is the College Level Examination Program (CLEP) of the College Board. A less standardized process for documenting prior learning has been encouraged and supported by the Council for Adult and Experiential Learning (CAEL). A large number of colleges now provide for individual evaluations of previous learning, using a portfolio created by the learner and evaluated by appropriate faculty.

Institutions known as "external degree" programs help students take advantage of nontraditional forms of learning. Such programs have no traditional campus, but rather serve as clearinghouses to document prior learning, credit previous coursework, and certify mastery in prescribed areas. Examples of these institutions include Empire State College and Thomas Edison College (Rose, 1989).

Experiential Applications for Personal Development and Classroom-based Learning. A third area of interest within higher education has been classroom-based experiential learning. During the 1980s, reformers of education looked to experiential education as an antidote for traditional education, which was under attack for being passive and concerned solely with transferring already assimilated knowledge from teacher to student.

Experiential learning in the classroom was given a boost when Chickering and Gamson (1987) recommended "active learning" as one of the seven "principles of good practice" for excellence in undergraduate education. Active learning in the classroom requires that students do more than just listen. To qualify as active, educational practices must involve students in doing things and thinking about what they are doing.

Role plays, games, case studies, critical incidents, simulations such as "in box" exercises, socio-drama, and values clarification exercises are some of the many forms of experiential learning techniques currently in use. In experiential classrooms, students can process real-life scenarios, experiment with new behaviors, and receive feedback in a safe environment. Experiential learning assignments help students relate theory to practice and analyze real-life situations in light of course material.

Some practitioners are currently advocating the use of Kolb's model to guide instructional design for college classrooms. Claxton (1990) describes a variety of teaching techniques that will foster each of Kolb's learning modes. Concrete experiences can be evoked by recalling past experiences, through role play, or via case studies; reflective observation is cultivated by group discussions, reflective papers, and journals; abstract conceptualization is stimulated by lectures, print sources, and films; and active experimentation is often encouraged by means of problem-solving exercises such as mock proposals or role plays. Claxton recommends that instructional designs include all four kinds of learning, which in turn help to ensure a complete cycle of learning with the capacity to elicit changed behavior at a more complex level of functioning.

Kolb's experiential model, by encouraging the four different modes of learning, is also more likely to engage gender-related learning style preferences (Claxton, 1990). Belenky, Clinchy, Goldberger, and Tarule's (1986) book *Women's Ways of Knowing* supports this notion by contrasting two different ways of knowing. What they call *separate knowing* emphasizes previously articulated knowledge and requires a separation of the knower from the object of study. In contrast, *connected knowing* requires a personal acquaintance with "the thing" being studied. The authors recommend that educational practice integrate both ways of knowing. Claxton (1990) finds a parallel between Kolb's concrete experience and the concept of connected knowing, and between abstract conceptualization and separate knowing. Thus, the teaching methodology recommended by Belenky and others, and the instructional design extrapolated from Kolb, are congruent and offer the possibility of more efficient and complete learning.

A growing number of professionals consider adult, continuing, and higher education responsible for prompting the development of students and preparing them for lifelong learning. By stretching the learner's ability to deal with moral complexity, experiential learning becomes a vehicle for adult development by helping learners reach new levels of cognitive, perceptual, behavioral, and symbolic complexity. Chickering (1981, p. 2) refers to adult development as "the unifying idea" of higher education. As we have noted, theorists who believe in the transformational power of learning view critical reflection on experience as the key to development.

Great potential for meaningful learning is inherent in experiential learning. However, learning goals have not always been clearly articulated nor learning outcomes assessed by educators. In higher education, experiential learning exercises often are not integral to course goals and thus are not evaluated. Further, students' incidental learning, which can be significant, is often not recognized or valued in formal classroom settings. The current emphasis on experiential learning in continuing higher education and the move toward assessing student outcomes provide a beneficial climate for refining experiential approaches.

Similar attention is now being focused on experiential strategies within the corporate sector. Notions of the learning organization and total quality management have given rise to a myriad of training programs designed to embed such concepts throughout entire organizations. Unlike colleges and universities, corporations are usually less confined by convention and are more willing to experiment with promising experiential approaches.

The following section details examples of state-of-the-art strategies currently in place in leading-edge companies and forward-thinking organizations. Each should be scrutinized by practitioners, educators, and administrators alike as possible templates for the development of similar experiential learning opportunities in a variety of learning environments.

Current Applications of Experiential Learning in the Workplace

Each year the government and employers in private for profit and private non-profit sectors make a significant monetary commitment to training and employee development. Organizations with 100 or more employees spent over $45 billion on formal training in 1992. Estimates of U.S. employers' actual total training investment including informal and on-the-job training are estimated to be in the $200 billion range (Lee, 1992).

These expenditures are fueled by ever-increasing demands for employee accountability and a need to document how training influences bottom-line results. Employers dedicate a substantial portion of training investments to developing managers, spending approximately 1 percent of revenues for management education (Bolt, 1987). While many of these programs are subject-matter–centered and focus on specific objectives, there is also a heavy emphasis on experiential learning that presents intellectual, psychological, and even physical challenges.

Experiential models are being applied more widely than ever before in business and industry because experiential learning legitimizes acquiring self-knowledge. Learners now have a mandate to see, learn about, and examine their own unique situations in action as they interact with others at work.

Three popular forms of experiential learning—action learning, future search and outdoor education—are described in the following sections. Each of these current applications requires learners to engage in the four types of learning specified by Kolb: (1) get involved fully and openly in new experiences; (2) reflect on and interpret these experiences from different perspectives; (3) create concepts and ideas to integrate their observations logically; and (4) use their learning and newly derived theories to make decisions, solve problems, and meet new challenges.

Action Learning. In today's business world training for training's sake is an unaffordable luxury. As a result, leading-edge companies are turning to action learning, a hybrid technique that allows participants to use what they learn to tackle priority problems within their companies under actual work conditions. Action learning is a social process for resolving the difficulties managers increasingly confront, where history offers no solution.

At its heart, action learning is a systematic process that increases participants' organizational learning in order to help them respond more effectively to change. Originated by Reg Revans (1983), action learning is based on the underlying premise that there is no learning without action and no action without learning. Action learning is inextricably linked with action science. Action science (Argyris, Putnam, and Smith, 1985) provides a conceptual framework and a methodology for facilitating action learning, while Revan's work establishes the actual form. The following processes of action science are implicit in action learning:

Critical reflection: bringing underlying assumptions to consciousness; testing those assumptions to determine if they are appropriate for attaining the desired goal
Reframing: altering assumptions that don't accomplish desired goals
Unlearning and relearning: developing new sets of learned skills based on reframed assumptions; replacing old with new skills until new ones are automatic.

Action learning methodology has three main elements: problems that people identify; people who accept responsibility for taking action on a particular issue; and colleagues who support and challenge one another in the process of resolving the problems. Using real tasks as the vehicle for learning, individuals, groups, or teams develop management and leadership skills while working on organizational problems and testing their assumptions against real consequences. By taking a real problem, analyzing it, and implementing solutions derived with colleagues, individuals monitor results and can be held accountable for their actions. Revans believes that if we are to cope with accelerating and turbulent change, then we must place our confidence in the lived experiences and insights of others in order to be successful.

Certain criteria characterize action learning. First, there must be a real and urgent need to solve an unfamiliar problem that is not necessarily amenable to an expert solution. For example, how can the organization be redesigned to eliminate waste and allow managers to run the business as if it were theirs? Under the auspices of a sponsor who nominates participants, as well as a client who defines the problem, participants diagnose, offer solutions, and implement action plans.

Action learning is much more ambiguous than standard classroom-based experiences. Instead of being able to rely on experts for answers, individuals must engage in just-in-time learning—opportunities to develop knowledge and understanding at the appropriate time based on immediate felt needs. This requires strong internal support and the ability to ground training in business requirements. Participants must identify and access different stakeholders and internal functional experts throughout the process. In addition, formal training modules are delivered by topic specialists. However, most critical to the process is involvement by a facilitator—someone who can act independently of the corporate culture to assist teams in reflecting on their own actions and resolving conflicts. Internal strife sometimes occurs within organizations as individuals are affected by resolution of a problem.

Multiple benefits accrue from action learning. Participants not only gain self-understanding and skills but also uncover the real reasons underlying existing problems. As organizations, institutions, and businesses seek to manage constant change, action learning should be considered as a significant intervention that has limitless potential.

Future Search. While standard approaches to professional development often consist of attending traditional business conferences or listening to charismatic speakers or best-selling authors, Future Search is a highly participatory process that helps individuals and organizations respond to the psychological stresses of accelerated change. Dating back to the early 1960s, the strategy grew out of an actual managerial dilemma posed by a pending merger (Weisbord, 1992). Through collaborative inquiry, a group of managers undertook an intense, week-long marathon dialogue on the changes confronting them, both in the world, their industry, and their own company. As a result, managers made crucial choices and invented new ways of doing business.

Today, in its most commonly applied format, a Future Search Conference is a three-day event, involving up to 60 participants from the same organization. Attendees collaborate to create a common vision by drawing on history, identifying desirable and undesirable practices, and defining the values for a desired future (Weisbord, 1992). The Future Search process is not about problem solving, but rather an exercise in developing insights, understanding, learning from one another, reducing misunderstandings, raising commitment, and uncovering new possibilities.

Throughout the process, individuals engage in a series of structured tasks. A cross-section of individuals with a stake in the sponsoring organization's future are drawn from as many functions and levels as feasible. The greater the diversity of views, experience, and knowledge, the greater the likelihood of creative solutions.

Initially, people examine their collective past, recalling and recording significant events and milestones using memorabilia such as photos, awards, and brochures that capture the organization's history. Through reflection, people identify good and bad trends, discover guiding principles, and highlight the values and actions that shaped the organization's earlier directions and previous practices.

Thereafter, attention is on the present. The focus is on external events and trends currently affecting the future. Participants generate a list of "prouds" and "sorries"—the things that are going on in their organizations about which they feel good or bad. As individuals vote for their proudest "prouds" and saddest "sorries," an appreciation of strengths and needs as well as an admission of weaknesses and mistakes emerges. These activities enable participants to gain new insights as they share perspectives, identify common themes, and conceptualize new behaviors.

In the final stage participants generate future images by imagining the most desirable and attainable future with a five-year horizon. People reflect on what they have learned and suggest actions for themselves, their work units, and the whole organization.

This process is successful because it involves people in creating their own future, taps their own experiences, and allows them to plan present actions by working backwards from what is really desired (Weisbord, 1992). The ability to make strategic choices, grounded in life experiences, fosters commitment. Future Search is an event for getting whole systems together in one room, and its success is predicated on a highly participative process for discovery learning. Whether the need is to reposition a business or to downsize, people tend to commit to plans they help to develop.

Outdoor Education. Many organizations, anxious to build teamwork, turn to outdoor physical challenge activities as a way to promote risk-taking, improve communication, and increase the productivity of intact work groups. Sometimes referred to as executive challenge or outdoor management training, outdoor experiential learning is driven by process, not content. In 1991, major market employers spent more than $277 million on outdoor programs in the hope of developing better managers (Laabs, 1991).

Because individuals and groups often behave the same way whether in the wilderness or in the office, outdoor education becomes a metaphor for organizational behavior. By analyzing what goes wrong during an outdoor experience, individuals gain insights as to what may be impeding progress back at their offices. Guided by an experienced facilitator, participants analyze, interpret, and gain new understandings from the strong emotional experiences they encounter through challenge activities. As the power of these experiences comes from the insights drawn from them, sponsors and facilitators must be clear about the objectives and goals to be accomplished through such programs. Unless there is agreement initially on what problems the program is to address, facilitators can process any aspect of the experience and miss important elements related to the group's unique organizational issues.

Throughout the process, a facilitator is responsible for introducing content into the program as appropriate and for helping participants analyze, interpret, and gain new insights through debriefing sessions. Teamwork and valuing of diverse viewpoints are fostered. For example, if a team has difficulty traversing a stream to rescue a colleague, a problem-solving model could be introduced to evaluate performance or structure future behavior and actions. Second and third attempts to solve similar challenges then provide practice opportunities to actively experiment with the newly found problem-solving skills and models.

A comprehensive study of six companies and over 1,200 employees suggests that the success of such programs is not related to the amount of time spent outdoors or to the particular setting, but rather to the process that facilitates behavior changes (Wagner and Roland, 1992). While expectations of personality transformation are unrealistic, participant reports consistently show significant improvement in the overall functioning of a work group but no significant changes in individual behavior after attending a program (Wagner and Roland, 1992).

The implicit assumption underlying outdoor programs is that team members will apply their new learning upon returning to the job. Skepticism about the long-term effectiveness and payoffs of these very costly programs emanates from the fact that without ongoing facilitation and debriefing back in the work environment, individuals revert to old ways of interacting. Since there is a dearth of hard evidence on the effectiveness of outdoor programs in general, it is essential that designers, deliverers, and purchasers work together to assess which specific goals can be reached through this approach.

Final Reflections

All of the experiential techniques described in this chapter share several characteristics. Each is intended to encourage investigation and open-mindedness and to promote practice with important, previously identified skills and behaviors. Each mode inspires questions and encourages viewing issues from various perspectives based on others' input. Yet the practical applications to real-life situations are considered the responsibility of the learner.

Action learning, Future Search, and outdoor education integrate thought and action with reflection. However, while reflective practice influences professional growth, experiential strategies are often costly, time-consuming, and involve varying degrees of personal risk. As learners engage in ambiguous and complex learning situations, they confront conflicting values and gaps between theory and practice. Their personal feelings, philosophy, and even their professional practices are called to question. In addition, potential disruptions and the uncertainty about which course of action to take often deter even experienced professionals from using experiential strategies.

Because the nature of work is changing so radically and rapidly, a paradigm shift from a training to a learning emphasis is essential so that people are equipped to deal with new, unspecified challenges. More than ever before it is important to implement experiential designs that encourage individuals to become continuous learners, to extract meaning from their experiences, and to pass the learning along in collaborative contexts.

Requiring learners simply to engage in experience is not enough. Experiences, whether field-based, simulated, or on the job, must be processed through reflection and debriefing in order to maximize their value. There is also an ongoing need for better research about experiential learning. Most published articles on experiential learning are descriptive accounts. Few offer evidence that learners actually acquire targeted skills. Only programs that have clear objectives, skilled facilitation, and credible evaluation will be effective and respected. And only if educators can demonstrate meaningful learning will the corporate sector be willing to invest in expensive experiential learning programs. Those programs that have been successfully utilizing experiential learning for a number of years must be identified as exemplary models. A new approach to experiential learning, such as that described in this volume, can serve as an alternative framework for others to adapt.

It is becoming increasingly important that adult learners know how to learn and assume responsibility for their own learning. The rapid pace of change today demands lifelong learning. People can become better learners by acquiring a repertoire of attitudes, skills, and understandings that allow them to become more effective, flexible, and self-organized learners in a variety of contexts.

In the chapters that follow, the contributing authors to this volume expand upon the experiential models presented herein. Each recognizes the unlimited potential that exists for developing innovative, yet highly relevant experiential approaches to a variety of learning environments for adults. The challenge for practitioners is to experiment and continue to search for new and better ways of encouraging reflection in action.

References

Argyris, C., Putnam, R., and Smith, D. M. *Action Science*. San Francisco: Jossey-Bass, 1985.

Belenky, M. F., Clinchy, B. M., Goldberger, N. R., and Tarule, J. *Women's Ways of Knowing: The Development of Self, Voice and Mind*. New York: Basic Books, 1986.

Bolt, J. F. "Trends in Management Training and Executive Education: The Revolution Continues." *Journal of Management Development*, 1987, 6 (5), 5–15.

Chickering, A. W. "Introduction." In A. W. Chickering and Associates (eds.), *The Modern American College: Responding to the New Realities of Diverse Students and a Changing Society*. San Francisco: Jossey-Bass, 1981.

Chickering, A. W., and Gamson, Z. F. "Seven Principles for Good Practice in Undergraduate Education." *AAHE Bulletin*, 1987, 3–7.

Claxton, C. S. "Learning Styles, Minority Students and Effective Education." *Journal of Developmental Education*, 1990, 14 (1), 6–8, 35.

Dewey, J. *Experience and Education*. New York: Collier Books, 1971. (Originally published 1938.)

Freire, P. *Pedagogy of the Oppressed*. New York: Seabury Press, 1970.

Habermas, J. *Knowledge and Human Interests*. Portsmouth, N.H.: Heinemann Educational Books, 1972.

Kolb, D. A. *Experiential Learning: Experience as the Source of Learning and Development*. Englewood Cliffs, N.J.: Prentice Hall, 1984.

Kolb, D. A., and Lewis, L. H. "Facilitating Experiential Learning: Observations and Reflections." In L. H. Lewis (ed.), *Experiential and Simulation Techniques for Teaching Adults*. New Directions for Continuing Education, no. 30. San Francisco: Jossey-Bass, 1986.

Laabs, J. J. "Team Training Goes Outdoors." *Personnel Journal*, June 1991, 70, 56–63.

Lee, C. "The Budget Blahs." *Training*, 1992, 29 (10), 31–38.

Mezirow, J. D. "A Critical Theory of Adult Learning and Education." *Adult Education*, 1981, 32 (1), 3–24.

Mezirow, J. D. "Conclusion: Toward Transformative Learning and Emancipatory Education." In J. Mezirow and Associates, *Fostering Critical Reflection in Adulthood: A Guide to Transformative and Emancipatory Education*. San Francisco: Jossey-Bass, 1990.

Revans, R. W. *The ABC of Action Learning*. Bromley, England: Chartwell-Brathl, 1983.

Rose, A. D. "Nontraditional Education and the Assessment of Prior Learning." In S. B. Merriam and P. M. Cunningham (eds.), *Handbook of Adult and Continuing Education*. San Francisco: Jossey-Bass, 1989.

Tisdell, E. J. "Feminism and Adult Learning: Power, Pedagogy, and Praxis." In S. B. Merriam (ed.), *An Update on Adult Learning Theory*. New Directions for Adult and Continuing Education, no. 57. San Francisco: Jossey-Bass, 1993.

Wagner, R. J., and Roland, C. C. "How Effective is Outdoor Education?" *Training and Development Journal*, July 1992, *46*, 61–62.

Weisbord, M. R. *Discovering Common Ground*. San Francisco: Berrett-Koehler, 1992.

LINDA H. LEWIS *is vice president of corporate education for Travelers Companies, Hartford, Connecticut.*

CAROL J. WILLIAMS *is associate dean of the School of Continuing Education at Eastern Connecticut State University.*

A process model is described that links the needs of adult learners and conceptual issues in experiential learning with methods for engaging learners in experiential learning activities and authentic assessment practices.

Introduction to a New Approach to Experiential Learning

Lewis Jackson, Doug MacIsaac

Linda Lewis and Carol Williams (Chapter One) provide ample evidence that the field of experiential learning has made significant strides in redefining and reconceptualizing the learning needs and knowledge acquisition processes of adult learners. Coupled with rapid and complex changes in the workplace and in societal values, advances in experiential learning challenge traditional instructional and assessment practices, bringing into question their utility, their effectiveness, and their representation of relevant learning outcomes (Brookfield, 1992; Candy, 1991; Mezirow, 1990). There is apparent need to continue developing models that approach adult learning from an experiential learning orientation and provide conceptual underpinnings for the many changes that are occurring in our perspectives on teaching and learning.

In this chapter we present an overview of a descriptive model of experiential learning. First we offer four issues, drawn from Chapter One, that should be considered when constructing a model of teaching and assessment from an experiential learning perspective. We then introduce and describe the experiential learning model and its five major components. Finally, we elaborate on the model components and identify subsequent chapters in this volume that provide comprehensive discussions of each component.

Four Issues Relevant to Model Development

Four issues can be drawn from Chapter One (Lewis and Williams) that are especially relevant to the development of a contemporary model of experiential learning processes and outcomes. First, expectations of the education community, the corporate sector, and of society at large place a premium on preparing learners who are flexible and who can utilize pre-existing skills and knowledge in new and varied ways. This expectation obligates educators of adults to closely examine the nature and needs of adult learners—their unique backgrounds, experiences, learning styles, social affiliation patterns, and the contexts of their lives as they relate to educational, occupational, and personal life aspirations.

Second, the way we conceptualize learning has changed significantly. This change reflects a shift in our view of the nature of knowledge and the processes of knowledge acquisition—from knowledge as "conclusive and objective" to knowledge as "tentative and socially constructed," and from knowledge acquisition as learning units of information and basic skills to knowledge acquisition as gaining "in-depth understanding" and critical thinking skills (Newmann, 1993, p. 11).

Third, the methods and techniques associated with experiential learning instruction are expanding exponentially. With respect to both classroom and field settings, there is an increasing use of instructional activities that employ action- and problem-oriented collaborative tasks that represent conditions and issues derived from real-world analogues. As highlighted in Lewis and Williams' discussion of the Future Search Conference, the emphasis is on preparing participants to deal proactively with future uncertainties for which there are no "fail-safe" solutions. Arguably, this approach to instruction stands in marked contrast to the emphasis of earlier periods on understanding "time honored knowledge of the past" as a basis for interpreting and responding to the future.

Fourth and finally, emerging approaches to teaching and learning require educators of adults (corporate training officers, university professors, staff development personnel) to revisit long-standing methods of performance assessment. Increasingly, concepts associated with traditional psychometric testing and competency-based assessment are being challenged because they fail to adequately represent the learning outcomes, or the performance potential, of learners who have completed a given learning activity or program (Cizek, 1993; Hanson, 1993).

The need for a comprehensive model that addresses and links these four issues—the characteristics and needs of the adult learner, the conceptual foundations of experiential learning, methods and techniques for engaging learners in experiential learning, and changing assessment practices—is predicated on two especially prominent concerns. First, it is imperative that the design and implementation of instructional programs for adults reflect an integration and synthesis of these four interrelated issues. As an illustration, consider programs that address the retooling needs of middle-aged women who are reentering the work force (Wolf, 1993). If such programs are to provide a valued and marketable service, they must conjointly consider the background knowledge and emotional/motivational needs of the individual participants, cognitive learning processes and their implications for instruction and outcome specification, the kinds of in-class and field-based experiences that promote experiential learning, and the types of assessment practices that simultaneously

measure immediate and long-term growth while promoting program participants in the job market.

Second, recent years have witnessed an explosion of ideas and techniques
for thinking about and engaging in experiential teaching and assessment practices. A coherent framework that identifies the properties of, and interrelationships between, these four issues can promote systematic validation research
into ongoing experiential learning practices that, at present, lack a strong
empirical base.

In the next section an experiential learning model that is compatible with
the aforementioned issues and concerns is introduced and described.

An Experiential Learning Model for Teaching and Assessment

Figure 2.1 illustrates our experiential learning model and its five components.
Within each component (the individual boxes) variables are identified that represent especially critical dimensions of the model components. For example,
the component "Methods and Techniques for Engaging Learners in Experiential Learning Activities" identifies three dimensions of application: in-class
experiences; field-based experiences (for example, internships, practicums, and
on-the-job experiences); and the coordination of in-class and field-based experiences. These can be viewed as three levels in which experiential learning concepts can be applied. Educators of adults can be working within a particular
level, or they can be responsible for coordinating activities at several levels.

The model, which is explained in more detail in the sections that follow,
is a *process model:* The operational sequence associated with the model's components is expressed in the directionality of the model. This sequence can
guide practitioners who are applying the model to tasks associated with conceptualizing and implementing instructional programs and activities for adults.

The sequence begins with two components that describe the characteristics and needs of adult learners and the conceptual foundations of experiential learning. As indicated by the X symbol, these two components must be
viewed concurrently when attempting to fully understand functional elements
of experiential learning.

The next component describes methods and techniques for engaging
learners in experiential learning activities. This component of the model
focuses on formal instructional programs designed for adult learners.

Finally, the model has two components that relate to assessment. The first
addresses the various tools of assessment, while the second relates to how these
tools can be viewed collectively in the process of evaluating what learners have
acquired from a program or related experiences. These two model components
offer the interrelated concepts of *folio* and *portfolio* construction as foundations
for both formally assessing learners and for promoting self-reflection.

In the following sections we elaborate on the five components of the
model that are shown in the figure and identify the specific chapters in which

Figure 2.1. Applying Experiential Learning in Teaching and
Assessment: A Process Model

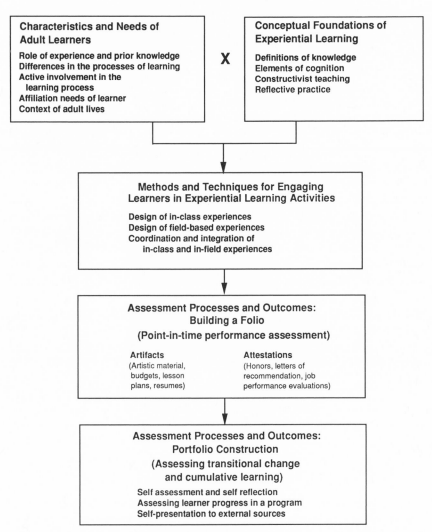

more details about each component are presented. Our discussion begins with
the characteristics and needs of adult learners.

Characteristics and Needs of Adult Learners. Persons participating in
adult and continuing education are a highly diverse group, and this diversity
reflects both our changing society and individual differences in experiences
and learning styles. With respect to our changing society, ongoing social, cultural, and occupational diversification are prominent features of modern life,
and programs for adult learners must be prepared to respond to and support
the resulting diversity in program participants. In the decade of the nineties,

individuals participating in workshops, training programs, and continuing education experiences will likely reflect an even wider range of ethnic and cultural backgrounds, age ranges, experiential histories, and professional needs than in past decades (Beziat, 1990; Hensel, 1991; Merriam and Caffarella, 1991; Ricard, 1991; Ross-Gordon, 1991; Merriam, 1993; Wolf, 1993). Revolutionary changes in the roles and responsibilities of persons within the work force will also require educators of adults to substantially reevaluate their consumers and their respective needs. For example, in some fields, traditional management hierarchies are being disassembled and replaced with more egalitarian structures (Villa, Thousand, Stainback, and Stainback, 1992; Holzman, 1993). Adults within these settings must significantly redefine their social and professional roles, responsibilities, and even their basic attitudes towards authority and power. Educational programs must therefore be responsive to these dramatic and potentially sweeping changes in the learning needs of adults in these types of work environments.

With respect to personal backgrounds and learning styles, both the information acquisition patterns of learners and aspects of their experiential history can be factors in how people respond to educational programs. For example, Endorf and McNeff (1991) describe five types of adult learners, each representing a complex interaction of learner histories and aspects of their personalities: *confident, pragmatic, and goal-oriented learners,* who are self-sufficient and need little peer support; *affective learners,* who are enmeshed in the feelings of the learning process and tend to view being in a program as a potentially exciting and pleasurable activity; *learners in transition,* who have not completely developed their plans and goals, and may show a preoccupation with questioning the value and utility of their selected educational pursuits; *integrated learners,* who have a clear vision of where they are going and tend to view a formal educational program as one small part of the broader range of life experiences that they are having; and *risk takers,* who tend to be adventurous, boldly changing their life's direction in the pursuit of new professional goals and learning opportunities.

Personal background also involves the unique cultural backgrounds of learners. A perspective on adult learners offered by Ricard (1991) brings into focus the way in which cultural differences with respect to thinking, valuing, speaking, listening, gesturing, and observing affect learning. Ricard provides a checklist that can be used by instructors to identify inter-learner differences, which then allows them to honor and respect these differences in their instruction. For example, because of cultural upbringing (or other factors), some learners prefer to be treated as equals while others are more comfortable with a formal learner-instructor status differential. As another example, some learners want to move quickly to the major points of a conversation, while others prefer a more indirect and meandering path from a conversation's opening to its critical content.

The above discussion clarifies that there are many unique ways to describe inter-individual differences in adult learners and their life contexts, and that knowledge of these differences can assist adult educators in configuring learning experiences so that they both respect individual differences and optimize learning in diverse groups of learners. This component of the model, "Characteristics and Needs of Adult Learners," identifies five dimensions for conceptualizing these issues: (1) *role of experience and prior knowledge,* which acknowledges that each learner possesses a unique experiential background that is, in and of itself, a resource that can be applied to new learning situations; (2) *differences in processes of learning,* which recognizes that each adult learner has a specific style of learning; (3) *active involvement in the learning process,* which requires learners to grasp the content of instruction, do things with it, and think about what they are doing; (4) *affiliation needs of learners,* which affirms the need for learners to be connected and supportive of each other's learning; and (5) *context of adult lives,* which recognizes that an adult's unique responsibilities and life situations affect learning. These variables are described in more detail by Caffarella and Barnett in Chapter Three.

Along with knowledge about the characteristics and needs of adult learners, persons who are designing and implementing instructional events and programs need to consider the conceptual foundations of experiential learning. This second component of the model is described in the next section.

Conceptual Foundations of Experiential Learning. Experiential learning does not represent a theory of learning per se. Rather, it is a broad perspective on learning that focuses on *authentic learning experiences* as the necessary basis for meaningful skill acquisition and human development. Two prominent properties of authentic learning experiences are described below.

First is the recognition that individuals do not simply absorb knowledge in authentic learning experiences, but they actively construct knowledge within the learning context. That is, learners utilize their prior knowledge in the interpretation, retention, and revision of incoming, new information. Broadly described across a variety of fields as *constructivism* (Candy, 1991; Marshall, 1992; Poplin and Stone, 1992; Jackson, Reid, and Bunsen, in press), this perspective on learning stresses that active participation in and active reflection on the learning process are essential features of successful learning. Knowledge acquisition from a constructivist framework is viewed as a nonlinear and dynamic process that is enhanced by problem-oriented and individualized approaches to instruction. The perspective also reinforces the importance of learner empowerment and self-directed learning with respect to identifying relevant learning opportunities and instructional outcomes.

Second is the recognition that learning is enhanced when features of the instructional context (such as qualities of the tasks that are used in instruction and the ecological setting in which instruction occurs) match or approximate relevant performance contexts. That is, to the extent that there are critical similarities between specific learning and specific performance contexts, transfer of learning, or the "effective application by . . . participants of what they learned as a result of attending an educational program," is optimized (Caffarella, in press, p. 279).

The component "Conceptual Foundations of Experiential Learning" identifies four dimensions that are consistent with the foregoing features of authentic learning experiences. These are (1) *definitions of knowledge,* which recognizes experiential knowing as an important form of knowledge for adult learners; (2) *elements of cognition,* which features two aspects of cognition (amount and nature of prior experience and knowledge, and situated cognition) as key ideas associated with the representation and retrieval of previously acquired information and experience; (3) *constructivist teaching,* which asserts that instructional activities must reflect awareness of how previously learned information influences new learning and how learners direct and control this process; and (4) *reflective practice,* which argues that the activity of recapturing an experience, thinking about it, mulling over it, and evaluating it is an essential ingredient in the experiential learning process (Boud, Keogh, and Walker, 1985). These variables are also expounded on in Chapter Three.

A working knowledge of the conceptual foundations of experiential learning, coupled with knowledge of the characteristics and needs of adult learners, provides a solid groundwork for designing and implementing instructional events and programs. The third component, the actual design for engaging learners in experiential learning activities, is described in the next section.

Methods and Techniques for Engaging Learners in Experiential Learning Activities. Philip Candy (1991) notes:

> It is impossible to say with certainty when teaching first occurred, but common sense would suggest that the very earliest forms of instruction were relatively informal and consisted of parents teaching their children or of people sharing with others in their family or tribal group insights about survival. . . . However, as the social complexity of human existence increased, . . . this then gave rise to more formal types of instruction. . . . It has been the practice to take some people aside to instruct them specifically in tasks and areas of knowledge considered vital to the continuation of the culture. [p. 202]

This passage aptly summarizes the dichotomy that can exist between informal, often "incidental" learning and formal instructional programs. Perhaps experiential learning can be described as an attempt to bridge the gap between formal and informal types of learning. Instructors design learning activities that capture aspects of informal and "natural" learning experiences, then deliver them under relatively controlled conditions (for example, in apprenticeships).

An emerging model of cultural learning provides insights that are applicable to bridging the gap between formal and informal forms of learning. Tomasello and Ratner (1993) suggest that a distinguishing feature of human social groups is the presence of *cultural learning,* which differs from other forms of learning in that the products of cultural learning can be continually modified over time. In other words, a learned practice (such as learning how to use a computer program, learning how to lay bricks, or learning the vocabulary of a language) can be transmitted to members of a group and across generations in a form that is increasingly different from its original form. This is the basis of progressive adaptation: As social, political, and economic conditions change, human traditions and rituals change as well. As the pace of change accelerates, as in modern society, the need for cultural revision becomes more apparent. This, in turn, places stress on the systems responsible for communicating cultural information to new generations of learners and to adults preparing for new roles and responsibilities.

Tomasello and Ratner describe a learning hierarchy that differentiates between three forms of learning, each of which involve a different relationship between learners and those responsible for their instruction. The first form of learning is *imitative learning:* Learners acquire needed information or skills by observing or listening to "masters" who are modeling the activity in vivo (Tomasello and Ratner, 1993, p. 497).

The second form of learning, which most closely resembles traditional classroom instruction, is *instructed learning:* Persons designated as "instructors" direct the skill and information acquisition processes of learners, while incidentally acquiring some new information from their learners during instructional interactions (Tomasello and Ratner, 1993, p. 497).

Finally, there is a third form of learning that is the richest form of cultural learning and the one most responsive to an accelerated rate of cultural change. This is *collaborative learning:* There is a sharing of information in relationships of equality that promotes new growth in each participant regardless of whether in the role of "instructor" or "learner." With respect to educating adults, this form of learning requires a redefinition of the role and status of the instructors from knowledge experts and knowledge providers to learning partners and learning facilitators (Tomasello and Ratner, 1993, p. 497).

Lee and Caffarella, in Chapter Four, explore activities of experiential learning that we believe capitalize on this emerging view of the relationship between learners and the persons responsible for instruction. As indicated in Figure 2.1, the third component of the model, "Methods and Techniques for Engaging Learners in Experiential Learning Activities," has three levels. First, participant engagement and subsequent learning depends on the design of the instructional activities used within individual classes, workshops, and the like (panels, games, debates, and so on). Second, engagement and learning is a function of the types of field-based learning that are provided to participants (practicums, internships, on-the-job coaching, mentorship, and so on). Third and finally, participant engagement and learning is a function of the coordination and integration of "in-class" and "field-based" experiences—that is, the specific configuration of sessions, workshops, classes, and so on, and field-based opportunities that participants complete as part of an educational program.

Enabling participants in an educational activity or program to perceive and reflect on the changes they are experiencing is an essential next step. This step depends on the assessment processes and outcomes that are selected to evaluate growth and change. Learner assessment also provides a mechanism for educators of adults to examine and reflect on the methods and techniques that they are using in instruction. The selection of assessment processes and outcomes comprises the fourth and fifth components of the model. Component four is described in the next section.

Assessment Processes and Outcomes: Building a Folio (Point-in-Time Performance Assessment). Gardner (1993) offers a useful contrast between two types of assessment: formal assessment, "an objective, decontextualized form of assessment, which can be adopted and implemented widely with some assurance that similar results will be obtained"; and apprenticement assessment, which can include a rich array of subjective and objective standards and expectations and "which is implemented . . . within a naturally occurring context in which the particulars of a craft are embedded" (p. 162). Modern society's emphasis on product uniformity has resulted in the former assessment model dominating assessment practices. Yet, the more flexible, contextually-situated, and individualized forms of assessment associated with the apprenticeship model are especially appropriate in experiential learning.

The formal assessment model is under broad attack on a number of practical and conceptual fronts. At a practical level, traditional assessment procedures, which often rely on indirect measures of learning (Whitney, 1993), are increasingly being recognized as, at best, inadequate and, at worse, misleading indices of occupation or task readiness. In contrast, apprenticement or *performance assessment* procedures implicitly recognize that the direct assessment of job or task performance gives a better indication of occupation or role readiness. As noted by Rickard, Stiles, Posey, and Eguez (1991), traditional tests may reveal what learners know, but they cannot reveal "how they will use what they know" (p. 10).

At a conceptual level, the issues being addressed are more weighty. In an important discussion of the social consequences of testing and normative assessment, Hanson (1993) asserts: "The two most important consequences of tests . . . is that they are mechanisms for defining or producing the concept of a person in contemporary society and that they maintain that person under surveillance and domination" (p. 3). In other words, formal tests do not simply mirror and describe qualities of a person; rather, they project and ascribe qualities *to a person.* Moreover, results from these kinds of tests (such as qualifying examinations and standardized aptitude tests) are then often used as a vehicle for test consumers to make life-affecting judgments on the opportunities and experiences that will or will not become available to a person. Moreover, the definitions of a person's competencies and failings will remain fixtures of a person's identity long after the testing process is over.

Presented in Chapter Five (Barnett and Lee) is the model component entitled "Assessment Processes and Outcomes: Building a Folio." This component, which emphasizes alternatives to formal testing procedures, offers assessment options that are especially useful in educational programs that endorse the goals and philosophies of experiential learning. As shown in the model figure, assessment options include *artifacts,* which are tangible products of the learning process (for example, a budget prepared as part of a family budgeting course) and *attestations,* which are documents prepared by others attesting to a person's skills, capabilities, or personal change experiences (for example, a letter of recommendation following completion of a secretarial program).

The assessment options described in the Barnett and Lee chapter are not only designed to assess immediate performance change; they also provide the basis for another component in the assessment process: portfolio construction. This is the fifth and final component of the model, which is described in the next section.

Assessment Processes and Outcomes: Portfolio Construction (Assessing Transitional Change and Cumulative Learning). Tibbetts and Keeton (1993) comment that we live "in an era of dramatic and often traumatic change and transition" (p. 7). Portfolio assessment represents an important emerging development in assessment because portfolios can support and promote learners in their passages through major adult transitions.

Portfolios are organized and visually pleasing collections of diverse products that provide evidence of a learner's growth and change (Jackson, Dobson, and Wimberley, 1992). Portfolios do not necessarily contain all of a learner's work; rather, they are selectively constructed from the broader array of artifacts, reproductions, and attestations that constitute the sum total of the folio. Portfolio construction is guided by the functions that are to be served by the finished collection of works. A dancer seeking employment in a musical drama company, for example, may organize a set of products and documents that reflect her skills as a singer, dancer, and actress; the same dancer may compose an entirely different portfolio if she were applying for a position as a dance teacher with a studio that serves young children. In other words, portfolios can be configured from a broader set of works in a manner that meets particular needs.

Portfolio assessment opens the possibility of at least three fundamental changes in the assessment activities that are typically employed in many instructional programs for adults. First, individual learners coming out of the same program may have different needs with respect to portfolio function; hence, programs that identify portfolios as one of their end products must provide expanded opportunities for self-direction and individualization in the assessment process. Second, portfolio assessment requires a values shift with respect to the purpose of learner assessment. Portfolios promote participants by displaying their strengths; they are not a means for documenting learner "deficits." Hence, the kinds of assessment artifacts that are included to illustrate skill changes need to be different from those often employed in more traditional learning programs in which the orientation is toward identifying and ameliorating skill "weaknesses" in learners. Third, portfolio assessment can be a dynamic process that continues across the life span. Therefore, portfolios should not be thought of as terminal products in a workshop, class, or program. Rather they should be viewed as reflections of ongoing transitions. Within this perspective, an instructional event or program becomes simply one of any number of life events that may be reflected in a portfolio.

The model component entitled "Assessment Processes and Outcomes: Portfolio Construction" is discussed in Chapter Six by MacIsaac and Jackson. As shown in the model figure, portfolio functions fall into three broad categories: portfolios for self-assessment, or reflection on personal growth; portfolios that facilitate progress assessment within an adult learning program; and portfolios that enhance self-presentation, such as a portfolio that can be applied to job search activities. In all cases, of course, portfolios portray cumulative learning; that is, the set of artifacts, reproductions, and attestations that are included in a portfolio give evidence to the evolving and expanding knowledge base and skill repertoire of the adult learner.

Conclusion

We have presented in this chapter an overview of a model of teaching, learning, and assessment that is consistent with ongoing trends in experiential learning and authentic assessment practices. As suggested at the start of this chapter, a major advance in experiential learning practices will have occurred when the design and implementation of educational programs for adult learners reflect an integration and synthesis of conceptual foundations of experiential learning, understanding of the characteristics and needs of the adult learner, experiential learning methods and techniques, and authentic assessment methodologies including learner folios and portfolios. The model presented here provides a framework for instructors in programs for adult learners to plan and design learning events and experiences that simultaneously consider all four of these issues. Illustrations of how to use this framework in business and industry and in higher education are provided in Chapter Seven by Bassett and Jackson.

References

Beziat, C. "Educating America's Last Minority: Adult Education's Role in the Americans with Disabilities Act." *Adult Learning,* 1990, 2 (2), 21–23.

Boud, D., Keogh, R., and Walker, D. "Promoting Reflection in Learning: A Model." In D. Boud, R. Keogh, and D. Walker (eds.), *Reflection: Turning Experience Into Learning.* New York: Kagan, 1985.

Brookfield, S. D. "Giving Helpful Evaluations of Learners." *Adult Learning,* 1992, 3 (8), 22–24.

Caffarella, R. S. *Planning Programs for Adult Learners: A Practical Guide for Educators, Trainers, and Staff Developers.* San Francisco: Jossey-Bass, in press.

Candy, P. C. *Self-Direction for Lifelong Learning: A Comprehensive Guide to Theory and Practice.* San Francisco: Jossey-Bass, 1991.

Cizek, G. J. "Rethinking Psychometricians' Beliefs About Learning." *Educational Researcher,* 1993, 22 (4), 4–9.

Endorf, M., and McNeff, M. "The Adult Learner: Five Types." *Adult Learning,* 1991, 2 (7), 20–22.

Gardner, H. *Multiple Intelligences: The Theory in Practice.* New York: Basic Books, 1993.

Hanson, F. A. *Testing, Testing: Social Consequences of the Examined Life.* Berkeley: University of California Press, 1993.

Hensel, N. "Accommodating the Needs of Adults in Teacher Education Programs." *Adult Learning,* 1991, 2 (6), 20–21, 25.

Holzman, D. "When Workers Run the Show." *Working Woman,* Aug. 1993.

Jackson, L., Dobson, D., and Wimberley, G. *Tools for Assessing Successful Inclusion.* Paper presented at the third annual Strategies for Integrated Education conference, Denver, Feb. 1992.

Jackson, L., Reid, D. K., and Bunsen, T. "Alternative Dreams: A Response to Felix Billingsley." *Journal of the Association for Persons with Severe Handicaps,* in press.

Marshall, H. H. "Seeing, Redefining, and Supporting Student Learning." In H. H. Marshall (ed.), *Redefining Student Learning: Roots of Educational Change.* Norwood, N.J.: Ablex, 1992.

Merriam, S. B. (ed.). *An Update on Adult Learning Theory.* New Directions for Adult and Continuing Education, no. 57. San Francisco: Jossey-Bass, 1993.

Merriam, S. B., and Caffarella, R. S. *Learning in Adulthood: A Comprehensive Guide.* San Francisco: Jossey-Bass, 1991.

Mezirow, J. *Fostering Critical Reflection in Adulthood: A Guide to Transformative and Emancipatory Learning.* San Francisco: Jossey-Bass, 1990.

Newmann, F. M. "Beyond Common Sense in Educational Restructuring: The Issues of Content and Linkage." *Educational Researcher,* 1993, 22 (2), 4–13.

Poplin, M. S., and Stone, S. "Paradigm Shifts in Instructional Strategies: From Reductionism to Holistic/Constructivism." In W. Stainback and S. Stainback (eds.), *Controversial Issues Confronting Special Education.* Needham Heights, Mass.: Allyn & Bacon, 1992.

Ricard, V. B. "How Effective Intercultural Communication Skills Can Support Learning." *Adult Learning,* 1991, 2 (5), 13–14.

Rickard, P. L., Stiles, R. L., Posey, V. K., and Eguez, J. B. "The Essential Role of Assessment." *Adult Learning,* 1991, 2 (7), 9–11.

Ross-Gordon, J. M. "Needed: A Multicultural Perspective for Adult Education." *Adult Education Quarterly,* 1991, 42, 1–16.

Tibbetts, J., and Keeton, P. "Transitions Are Here. Is Adult Education Ready?" *Adult Learning,* 1993, 4 (5), 7.

Tomasello, M., and Ratner, H. H. "Cultural Learning." *Behavioral and Brain Sciences,* 1993, 16, 495–552.

Villa, R. A., Thousand, J. S., Stainback, W., and Stainback, S. *Restructuring for Caring and Effective Education.* Baltimore: Paul Brookes, 1992.

Whitney, D. R. "Performance Assessment: Lessons from History." *Adult Learning,* 1993, 4 (3), 23–26.

Wolf, M. A. "Mentoring Middle-aged Women in the Classroom." *Adult Learning,* 1993, 4 (5), 8–10.

LEWIS JACKSON is associate professor in the Division of Special Education at the University of Northern Colorado.

DOUG MACISAAC is assistant professor in the Teacher Education Division at the University of Northern Colorado.

The knowledge bases of adult and experiential learning are viewed
as complementary to fully understanding how the functional elements
of the experiential learning model presented in this volume were
constructed.

Characteristics of Adult Learners and Foundations of Experiential Learning

Rosemary S. Caffarella, Bruce G. Barnett

In building this model of experiential learning, as discussed in the Editors' Notes, one of the major messages we are conveying is that effective instructors of adults must continually link conceptual and empirical knowledge about teaching and learning to how we actually teach and facilitate learning activities. This link must be a mutual exchange of ideas, observations, and critical reflection between and among practitioners and researchers on both what we teach (the content) and how and what we do to help adults learn (the process). It also may be a self-reflective exercise, combined with some peer observations, mentoring, or coaching for those of us who are involved simultaneously in the world of instructing adults and engaging in scholarly practice, such as college professors or graduate students who combine their professional roles as teachers, trainers, managers, and the like with the role of student.

The purpose of this chapter is to describe the conceptual and empirical knowledge base within which our model of experiential learning is grounded (see Components One and Two of Figure 2.1 in Chapter Two). Using a thematic framework, brief descriptions of the salient work in adult and experiential learning are given. Discussed first are important characteristics and needs of adult learners as described in the literature. This is followed by a review of the major conceptual foundations of experiential learning. Key references for those interested in further explorations of these two areas are given at the end of the chapter. As highlighted in Chapter Two (Jackson and MacIsaac), these two knowledge bases, illustrated by an *X* sign between the first two components of the model, must be viewed as complementary to fully understand how the functional elements of the model were constructed.

NEW DIRECTIONS FOR ADULT AND CONTINUING EDUCATION, no. 62, Summer 1994 © Jossey-Bass Inc., Publishers

Characteristics and Needs of Adult Learners

The first of the dual conceptual components of the model (see Figure 2.1), the characteristics and needs of adult learners, is grounded in the assumption that the model is primarily designed for use in instructional applications for adult learners. With further work and refinement, the model may have applications for learners of all ages, but our initial focus as a team has been twofold: (1) helping our colleagues to think about new approaches to experiential learning related to formal learning programs for adults; and (2) making changes in our own instructional practice to try out what for some of us are new ways of facilitating and assessing learning.

For experiential learning activities to be effective, educators and trainers must be cognizant of the characteristics and needs of adult learners. The three characteristics which have received the most attention in the literature are adults' need for the acknowledgment and use of their experiences and prior knowledge, the differing ways they go about learning, and their desire to be actively involved in the learning process versus being passive recipients of knowledge (Kidd, 1973; Knowles, 1980; Brookfield, 1986; Merriam and Caffarella, 1991; Merriam, 1993b). More recently, drawing primarily from the work related to women and learning, emphasis has also been placed on allowing the affiliation needs of learners to be addressed as a legitimate and vital component of the learning process in adulthood (Schneidewind, 1983; Belenky, Clinchy, Goldberger, and Tarule, 1986; Caffarella, 1992b; Tisdell, 1993). In addition, the complex content of adult lives has been highlighted as important to consider when exploring characteristics of adults as learners (Merriam and Caffarella, 1991; Merriam, 1993b). A brief description of each of these five major characteristics of adult learners, which must be considered in developing and assessing experiential learning activities for adult learners, is provided.

Role of Experience and Prior Knowledge. The comparatively richer life experiences and background of the adult has been cited by nearly all writers as a key factor in differentiating adult learning from child learning. In his seminal work on adult learning, Kidd (1973) notes that "adults have *more* experiences, adults have different *kinds* of experiences, and adult experiences are *organized differently*" (p. 46, emphasis in original). As accumulated life experiences differentiate children from adults, they also differentiate one adult from another. A group of seventy-year-olds, for example, usually has less in common than a group of twenty-year-olds.

Life experiences and use of prior knowledge function in several ways. First, as Knowles (1980) and Hiemstra and Sisco (1990) have observed, adult learners become important resources for learning. Adults can call upon their past experiences and prior knowledge in formulating learning activities, as well as serve as resources for each other during learning events. Experiential learning activities, such as reflective journals, critical incidents, and portfolio development, can provide opportunities to introduce adult learners' past and current experiences into the content of learning events (see Chapters Four and Six).

This can be a tricky business as adults often equate these experiences with who they are and therefore have a deep investment in them. The difficult part comes when instructors and learners challenge each other's experiences as "truth" for all, versus all parties accepting the use of learners' experiences as a point of departure for new learning and possible changes in thinking and practice.

Second, the need to make sense out of one's life experiences and what one knows as a result of those experiences is often an incentive for adults to engage in learning activities in the first place. For example, adults participate in workshops and support groups to assist them in coping with many life transitions such as divorce, illness, and death. In addition, adults are also motivated to return to learning activities by examining what is happening in their lives, even though the content of those activities does not have a direct connection to what is going on with their lives at present. This is exemplified by women and men who return to school to upgrade or learn new job skills as a result of a divorce or having the last of their children become more independent.

And third, in using and reflecting on their past experiences and prior knowledge, adults often both want and need to modify, transfer, and reintegrate what these experiences mean in terms of their values and beliefs, their storehouse of knowledge, and their skills and abilities (Daloz, 1986; Mezirow, 1991; Clark, 1993). Although this may be a difficult process for some, as noted earlier, it is often a fundamental part of the adult learning process (for example, in examining ways professionals function and learn, in changing personal attitude and belief systems, in fostering social change) (Baskett and Marsick, 1992; Cavaliere and Sgroi, 1992).

Differences in Processes of Learning. Each adult learner brings to the learning situation his or her own style of learning (Hiemstra and Sisco, 1990; James and Blank, 1993). Learning style is defined as a person's preferred way of processing information within specific learning situations. One way to describe learning style is by targeting through which senses learners appear to learn best. For example, some learn better through listening and reflecting, while others would rather visually see the material, and still others prefer to physically manipulate materials. Another way to think about learning style, as proposed by Endorf and McNeff (1991), described earlier in the Jackson and MacIsaac chapter (Chapter Two), is through the idea of learning types. Endorf and McNeff draw a picture of learning types as a complex interaction of learners' histories and personalities. These interactions lead to preferred differences in learning. For instance, some adults would rather learn in groups with a great deal of instructor direction, while others prefer to be more self-directed, even when working in groups.

There are a number of learning style inventories that can help adults become aware of their personal learning styles and their strengths and weaknesses as learners (James and Blank, 1993). What is helpful for adults in experiential learning situations is to have facilitators or instructors (1) assist learners in matching their preferred learning styles to learning techniques where such choices are available and (2) use a variety of learning techniques on a regular basis so that all learners feel their strengths are being tapped at different points in the process (see Chapter Four).

In addition, it should be noted that those who posit different stages of cognitive development at different ages have indicated that learning processes in adulthood may take on different dimensions (Riegel, 1973; Rybash, Hoyer, and Roodin, 1986; Labouvie-Vief, 1990; Kincheloe and Steinberg, 1993). Specifically, adults tend to be more reflective and dialectical in their thinking, that is, they appear to be more tolerant of contradictions and ambiguities, and they engage more often in problem finding as well as problem solving (Caffarella, 1992a). These suggested changes in ways of thinking for adults fit well the notion that the assessment procedures for experiential learning, and more specifically developing portfolios, should have a reflective component built into the process (see Chapter Six).

Active Involvement in the Learning Process. Most adults prefer to be actively involved in the learning process versus being primarily passive recipients of knowledge (Knowles, 1980; Silberman, 1990; Caffarella, 1992a). This does not mean that instructors give up the role of being information givers, but that their roles need to be expanded to include serving as resource advisors and learning facilitators (Brookfield, 1986; Hiemstra and Sisco, 1990). Acting as resource advisor includes assisting adults with the process of learning, such as helping them develop their own learning objectives and choose appropriate strategies for learning, as well as being a content resource. The role of content resource advisor involves sharing materials and experiences from the instructor's own array of resources and helping learners locate resources that can better be obtained from other sources (such as libraries, computerized data banks, other people). The facilitation role consists of organizing and serving as the process person for activities that use the participants' experiences as part of the learning process. There are numerous instructional techniques and strategies (see Chapter Four) for encouraging active learner participation in both in-class and field-based learning, from large and small group discussion to role plays and storytelling (Galbraith, 1990; Apps, 1991; Caffarella, in press).

Having learners be active participants in their own learning also demands, as noted in Chapter Two, that they may need to change how they have acted in terms of their roles as participants or students. Adult learners in formal programs can no longer assume that instructors have the only, or even the primary, responsibility for teaching them the material, but they too must take responsibility for their own learning. This responsibility can range from giving learners almost total control of the learning process through the use of individualized learning methods such as preparing learning contracts to having students give presentations in class to requiring them to take the initiative in finding mentors or peer coaches.

Affiliation Needs of Learners. Recognizing the affiliation needs of adult learners, namely the desire for learners to be connected and supportive of each other's learning, is an aspect of the learning process that has received more attention in the practice of teaching adults over the past five years. Although this practice has been addressed from a variety of perspectives, the most ardent voice for including the affiliation needs in teaching has come from discussion of women and the learning process (Belenky, Clinchy, Goldberger, and Tarule, 1986; Shrewsbury, 1987; Hayes, 1989; Collard and Stalker, 1991; Loughlin and Mott, 1992; Caffarella, 1992b). The common thread among these authors in responding to learners' needs to form relationships that encourage learning is the importance of collaborative inquiry, cooperative communication styles, and a holistic and democratic approach to learning. This collaborative way of knowing, coined by Belenky, Clinchy, Goldberger, and Tarule (1986) as "connected teaching," encourages a cooperative communication style between the instructor and the participants.

Collaborative teaching, based on the assumption that learners should be actively involved in the learning process, as described above, can be fostered in a number of ways. These include allowing learners to share in setting goals and objectives for the learning activities, giving learners the responsibility for carrying through some of the learning activities, using experiential teaching techniques, and providing opportunities for teamwork and projects. Examples of specific experiential structural techniques intended to foster collaborative learning include small group discussion, metaphor analysis, and case study analysis (see Chapter Four for a more complete discussion).

Creating a democratic process for learning is similar to the idea of promoting collaboration. Its hallmark is fostering an interactive participatory style with the dual goals of assisting learners in developing independence of thought and action as well as in creating create mutual or shared objectives (Shrewsbury, 1987). The democratizing of teaching recognizes that power and authority over the teaching process must be shared between instructors and learners in terms of making decisions about the learning experience as well as fostering a participatory style of learning. Examples of helpful resources for establishing this type of climate and structure for learning include materials by Knowles (1975, 1980) and Caffarella (in press) on program planning and learning contracts, Hiemstra and Sisco (1990) on individualizing instruction, Brookfield (1987) on developing critical thinking, and Hiemstra (1991) on creating effective learning environments.

Context of Adult Lives. Adults' unique responsibilities and life situations form a context that affects their learning. There are two principal contexts in which adults function: their personal context and the wider social context (Merriam and Caffarella, 1991; Merriam, 1993b). An adult's personal context consists of a person's history (where they have been), their current roles and responsibilities (where they are now), and their personal aspirations and dreams (where they would like to go). These personal images that adults carry around with them affect how they see themselves as learners. For example, adults who had difficulties in K-12 schooling often carry around internal pictures of themselves as poor learners and shy away when confronted with new learning experiences in formal settings. Even when these adults have been highly successful learners in self-directed or nonformal arenas, such as managing a home and family or negotiating job changes, this image of being a successful learner does not necessarily transfer to formal settings. On the other hand, learners who have been continually successful in formal schooling situations often fare much better in any type of formal learning environment. In contrast to the learners who conceive of themselves as unsuccessful "students" or learners, these adults often carry around with them past and present images of themselves as people who can handle formal learning situations, even when those situations are new or different from those they have experienced before.

Experiential learning techniques have the potential to capture the positive feelings adults have about themselves as learners as well as acknowledge and work with the negative perceptions. Experiential learning methods prove particularly powerful at the beginning of formal learning experiences for adults returning to higher education and other formal "schooling" sessions by helping those learners who perceive themselves as having little, if anything, to bring to those settings to visualize their strengths as learners from other life arenas, such as parenting, holding down a job, or learning hobbies or other self-directed projects. Techniques such as storytelling and journaling can be especially effective in helping learners gain insights into the strengths they bring to the learning situation.

The social context of adult learning also adds to our understanding of learning in adulthood. "What adults apparently 'choose' to learn, their access to learning opportunities, and, indeed, how they go about the learning process may be as much a function of the socioeconomic environment as individual mental processes" (Merriam, 1993a, p. 11). For example, when literacy programs became a more prominent part of workplace interest and responsibility, those programs became more accessible to full-time workers. These literacy programs often provide extra incentives such as a guarantee of better jobs and wages for those who successfully complete the program.

Discussions about the social context of adult learning have raised issues concerning the influence of social class, gender, ethnicity, cultural backgrounds, and political processes on adult learning, which for some adult educators have been important throughout the history of formal learning programs for adults (Stubblefield and Keene, 1989). These questions of differences among and between adult learners, grounded in the social context, are again being raised more vocally by writers and practitioners (for example, Jarvis, 1987, 1992; Hart, 1992; Welton, 1993; Tisdell, 1993). These issues raised by learner differences result in some difficult practice dilemmas if instructors truly want to address the realities of these issues in their learning situations. For example, are instructors willing to confront their own and their learners' behaviors and beliefs about how race, social class, and gender influence in-class interactions? Are instructors willing to change how and what they teach based on the cultural backgrounds and social experiences of their learners? Again one way to address this concern regarding how social context influences learning within formal learning situations is by using experiential learning techniques and authentic assessment practices. Asking learners to examine these issues in class situations through such methods as case studies and critical incidents, or in field settings through role assumption exercises, learner support groups, and clinical supervision, can be a powerful tool, as can the use of self-reflective portfolios (see Chapters Four and Six).

Conceptual Foundations of Experiential Learning

The second component of the model (see Figure 2.1), the conceptual foundations of experiential learning, focuses on the major ideas that undergird the practice of experiential learning. We have captured four dimensions that are consistent with the past and present literature on experiential learning: definitions of knowledge, elements of cognition, constructivist teaching, and reflective practice. Each of these dimensions is briefly reviewed in the following subsections, with key references for further study again cited at the end of the chapter.

Definitions of Knowledge. Knowledge in formal settings has often been equated with information giving by instructors. The image of teachers imparting knowledge to "students" as they take notes, ask questions, and possibly engage in some large and small group discussion tends to come to mind when learners are asked about formal learning situations. This image of teachers up front and learners in rows of chairs persists both in reality and in people's minds, even though using the learner's experience as part of the knowledge base has been promoted in adult learning programs for decades (for example, Kidd, 1973; Knowles, 1980).

Other forms of knowledge as legitimate in formal settings, and more specifically experiential knowledge, have been discussed by a number of authors. Schön (1983), Kolb (1984), and Boud, Keogh, and Walker (1985) are among the prominent writers who have challenged the way knowledge is constructed and used in professional and postsecondary settings. Schön, for example, viewed the experience of the learner as very important in the learning process. He coined the terms "knowing in action" and "reflection in action" to capture these ways of knowing. Knowing-in-action, often termed common sense, allows people to carry out actions and judgments without really having to think about them either prior to or during experience, such as driving a car or cooking dinner. Reflection-in-action is very different, in that people think about and change what they are doing while they are doing it—in essence "their thinking reshapes what they are doing" (Cervero, 1988, p. 44) while they are still engaged in the action. Both knowing-in-action and reflection-in-action are needed components of an experiential learning process. Kolb (1984), as described in the Lewis and Williams chapter (Chapter One), and Boud, Keogh, and Walker (1985) include concrete experiences of the learner as an important part of their models for learning.

More recently, Hart (1990) has highlighted experiential knowing as one of three major forms of knowledge—theoretical, empirical, and experiential. "Theoretical knowing encompasses the general or abstract principles of a body of facts, a science, or an art" (Hart, 1990, p. 156), while empirical knowledge is framed through confirming or disconfirming evidence collected through data-based studies. Experiential knowledge, according to Hart, is characterized as using one's personal experience and the experiences of others to inform the process of knowing. She highlights advantages of this form of knowing "as vividness, immediacy, and relevance" (Hart, 1990, p. 159), while its disadvantages lie in being "unrepresentative (a fluke), simplistic, and limiting" (p. 159). In using experiential knowledge, it is incumbent on instructors to capture the advantages, while ensuring that learners understand the limitations of that knowledge and couple it with other sources of knowing.

Elements of Cognition. Two aspects that are important to understanding the use of experiential learning with adults are (1) the amount and nature of prior experience and knowledge and (2) situated cognition. While we examined the role of prior experience and knowledge in learning earlier, two additional ideas are worth consideration: the breadth and depth of that experience and information, and the subject matter being explored. In terms of the amount of experience and knowledge one possesses, the difference between those who have a lot of experience and know a great deal about a subject (experts) and those who have very little experience and knowledge (novices) is a key distinction (Glaser, 1987; Chi, Glaser, and Farr, 1988). It appears that experts not only have a greater storehouse of knowledge and experience, but also think in different ways than novices. Novices interpret their experiences literally and in very concrete terms, while experts tend to organize their experiences around principles and abstractions. For example, adults who are constructing portfolios (see MacIsaac and Jackson, Chapter Six) and who are novices to an area of practice usually will need very specific instruction on how to define the purpose of the portfolio, what the various subsections of the portfolio should be, and what artifacts and attestations should be included. On the other hand, learners who have developed a number of portfolios will more likely have few problems identifying what their portfolios should contain and how they should be put together.

In further examination of the novice versus the expert learner issue, some have speculated that at least some learning processes, rather than being universal, may be specific to certain domains or subject matter—thus making transfer of learning across these domains very difficult, if not impossible, for many people (Shuell, 1986; Glaser, 1987; Chi, Glaser, and Farr, 1988). Some learners, for example, although very perceptive and advanced in their own fields of study, may have a great deal of trouble learning new subject matter that calls for different ways of thinking and being (for example, acceptance of diversity in the workplace).

The concept of situated cognition recognizes that "cognition is a social activity that incorporates the mind, the body, the activity, and the ingredients of the setting in a complex interactive and recursive manner" (Wilson, 1993, p. 72). Therefore this idea of situated cognition is foundational to experiential learning: learning activities need to be "situated" as closely as possible to practice they represent in order for learning transfer to become a reality. For example, learning decision making by comparing and contrasting different decision-making systems is a useful classroom exercise, but knowing about alternative systems for decision making does not necessarily transfer to using this information in real-world settings. Rather, it is helpful for learners to actually practice this skill on problems they are encountering in their work or personal lives, both in classrooms and ideally in real-life settings where they are making a variety of decisions. The more authentic the activity and the assessment of that activity, the more likely the person will be able to display that learning in actual practice. Specific examples of learning activities in which situated cognition is an integral part of learning programs include apprenticeships, internships, and on-the-job training. Other proposed models that use situated cognition as their grounding include cognitive apprenticeship (Brandt, Farmer, and Buckmaster, 1993) and anchored instruction (Wilson, 1993).

Constructivist Teaching. Those who teach from a constructivist perspective espouse that instructional planning, activities, and evaluation strategies must reflect how previously learned knowledge and experiences influence new learning. Learners may draw from a single experience new ideas and ways of thinking about one or multiple topics (Smith and McCormick, 1992). For example, an instructor may use a case study or role play to have students look at one facet of team building, such as building trust within a group. Or she could use this same case or role play to have learners explore a number of issues of working effectively within groups, from general interpersonal skills to conflict management. Instructors may also use a learner's multiple experiences for learning about one topic (Smith and McCormick, 1992). For example, a central issue that runs through many internship or practicum experiences is how to help learners become more reflective about their own practice.

Constructivist teaching allows learners to give meaning or "make sense out of the perplexing variety and constantly changing texture of their experiences" (Candy, 1989, p. 98). This type of teaching assumes that learners are active knowers who participate in their construction of knowledge, and it posits that novelty and change are part of most learning situations. The aim of teaching from this framework is not just transmitting knowledge, but negotiating meaning embedded in the multifaceted realities that students bring with them to learning experiences (Candy, 1989, 1991). Those who teach from a constructivist perspective also recognize that values are a critical part of inquiry, and therefore teachers must help learners understand what they value and how these values influence and frame the learning experience.

Pressley, Harris, and Marks (in press) stress that there are a number of variations on how instructors choose to operationalize constructivist teaching, from using discovery and exploration methods entirely to using extensive modeling and explanations. Examples of techniques for constructivist teaching with adults, which are explored further in Chapter Four (Lee and Caffarella), include case study analysis, critical incident techniques, reflective writing, and simulations and role playing (Galbraith, 1990; Brookfield, 1986). A word of caution here for instructors: Giving learners the opportunity to give meaning to their own experiences may not always be a positive process for learners or instructors (McCormick, 1990). Thinking about prior experiences through new frames or lenses may bring forth painful feelings, and in group learning situations often conflicting ideas, opinions, and feelings emerge. For example, in examining their reactions to ethical dilemmas they have faced in their work or personal lives, learners may find the feelings associated with those dilemmas intensely negative and very difficult to discuss. Often learners who have taken what they believe are strong ethical stances will talk about their feelings of vulnerability, aloneness, anger, and the like when asked to examine what they have learned about being ethical in their behavior and actions. These kinds of feelings are not easy for either the learner or the instructor to process. Care must be taken that learners are given the time and support they need to work through what this new learning is all about—what new or altered meanings they have brought to their past experiences.

Again it must be stressed that instructors who teach from the constructivist perspective must be willing to meet learners where they are in the learning process and be willing to journey with them to make meaning from their prior knowledge and experiences, whether that journey is pleasant, uncomfortable, or extremely painful. This calls for instructors to accept that sometimes, if not often, in the instructional process, the learners rather than the instructor will be in control of the process. Where learners want to venture with the process may be very different from where the instructor originally thought they should go. This can be disconcerting to both instructors and learners who carry with them expectations that the road to knowing should be carefully planned and executed, especially in formal learning settings.

Reflective Practice. Reflective practice is defined as the process of bringing past events to a conscious level and of determining appropriate ways to think, feel, and behave in the future. Through reflection, using what Schön (1983) refers to as an "internal dialogue with one's self," people use experience, intuition, and trial-and-error thinking to define, solve, or rethink a particular problem or dilemma they may be facing or have faced. Reflection can focus on a variety of issues, including the tacit norms underlying a judgment, the strategies behind an action, the feelings associated with an event, or the specific role a person is trying to fulfill.

There are a number of models for reflective thought and action (for example, Schön, 1983; Kolb, 1984; Mezirow, 1991; and Tremmel, 1993). As noted in the Lewis and Williams chapter (Chapter One), the Kolb model has been highly influential in framing how practitioners think about reflective practice. For example, Kolb's four-part reflective cycle, as described in Chapter One, is often used as the basis for teachers and administrators in public schools to reflect on their behaviors and decisions (Osterman and Kottkamp, 1993). Barnett (1989) has extended Kolb's model to include a fifth stage, that of planning for implementation (a plan of action for the future), which he inserts between

Kolb's stages of abstract conceptualization and active experimentation. His thinking in adding this fifth element to the model is that "without this step, people might not act on any insights gained in the abstract conceptualization phase" (Barnett, 1989, p. 6). Barnett goes on to outline five specific features of this plan: "a rationale for undertaking the plan, specific activities that will occur, other people who will be involved, a timeline of events and activities, [and] types of data to be collected to determine how the plan is working" (p. 6). Schön's notions of being a reflective practitioner, as outlined earlier in this chapter, have also been applied widely in practice (Cervero, 1988; Schön, 1991; Short and Rinehart, 1993). Schön (1991), as editor of a recent book, *The Reflective Turn,* has brought together a series of examples from "participatory action research" to "psychoanalytic approaches to reflection on practice" to illustrate how his ideas have been used.

Mezirow (1991) views reflection as a "process of critically assessing the content, process, or premise(s) of our efforts to interpret and give meaning to an experience" (p. 104). Through this process we look at both our actions and thoughts as problem solvers and problem posers. Mezirow (1991) has outlined an elegant and elaborate scheme for a "process of reflective action" which "begins with posing a problem and ends with taking action" (p. 108). Again as with other models, the emphasis is on action as the end product of the reflective process.

More recently, Tremmel (1993) has asked us to rethink how we operationalize the reflective process, from a linear model which is set in motion by a problem or a dilemma to one of being "mindful" of what is going on around us—"When one is mindful, one lives in the present and pays attention" (p. 444) to that present. He views paying attention to the present as both "paying attention not only to what is going on around us, but also within us" (p. 447). Tremmel's premise is that as educators we need to assist learners to be mindful of what they are thinking and feeling during the reflective process and to use those free-flowing thoughts and feelings as the point of departure for reflection versus a specific event or problem.

There are numerous ways to assist learners in becoming more reflective in their practice, such as journal writing, metaphor analysis, storytelling, and portfolio development (Brookfield, 1987; Mezirow and Assoc., 1990; Schön, 1991; Tremmel, 1993; "Promoting Reflection to Improve Practice," 1994). Again, these and other appropriate methods for helping learners tap into their experience in a reflective way are described in Chapters Four, Five, and Six of this volume.

Summary

We have presented in this chapter an overview of the conceptual and empirical knowledge bases which ground our model of experiential learning. As stressed earlier in this volume and again in this chapter, the major themes and ideas discussed in this chapter help us frame our model of experiential learning and determine how the model should be applied. Our strong belief is that consistency between theory and practice in building experiential learning opportunities into our formal adult learning programs is necessary. Instructors need to demonstrate this consistency and help learners maintain this consistency as they use experiential learning as one way of knowing and learning about themselves, other people, the organizations in which they function, and society in general.

References

Apps, J. W. *Mastering the Teaching of Adults.* Malabar, Fla.: Krieger, 1991.

Barnett, B. "Reflection: The Cornerstone of Learning from Experience." Paper presented at the annual convention of the University Council for Educational Administration, Scottsdale, Ariz., 1989.

Baskett, H.K.M., and Marsick, V. J. (eds.). *Professionals' Ways of Knowing: New Findings on How to Improve Professional Education.* New Directions for Adult and Continuing Education, no. 55. San Francisco: Jossey-Bass, 1992.

Belenky, M. F., Clinchy, B. M., Goldberger, N. G., and Tarule, J. M. *Women's Ways of Knowing.* New York: Basic Books, 1986.

Boud, D., Keogh, R., and Walker, D. (eds.). *Reflection: Turning Experience into Learning.* New York: Kagan Page, 1985.

Brandt, B. L., Farmer, J. A., and Buckmaster, A. "Cognitive Apprenticeship Approach to Helping Adults Learn." In D. D. Flannery (ed.), *Applying Cognitive Learning Theory to Adult Learning.* New Directions for Adult and Continuing Education, no. 59. San Francisco: Jossey-Bass, 1993.

Brookfield, S. *Understanding and Facilitating Adult Learning: A Comprehensive Analysis of Principles and Effective Practices.* San Francisco: Jossey-Bass, 1986.

Brookfield, S. *Developing Critical Thinkers: Challenging Adults to Explore Alternative Ways of Thinking and Acting.* San Francisco: Jossey-Bass, 1987.

Caffarella, R. S. "Cognitive Development in Adulthood." Paper presented at the annual conference of the Project for the Study of Adult Learning, Chicago, Ill., 1992a.

Caffarella, R. S. *Psychosocial Development of Women: Linkages to the Practice of Teaching and Learning in Adult Education.* Columbus, Ohio: ERIC Clearinghouse on Adult, Career, and Vocational Education, 1992b.

Caffarella, R. S. *Planning Programs for Adult Learners: A Practical Guide for Educators, Trainers, and Staff Developers.* San Francisco: Jossey-Bass, in press.

Candy, P. C. "Constructivism and the Study of Self-Direction in Adult Learning." *Studies in the Education of Adults,* 1989, *21,* 95–116.

Candy, P. C. *Self-Direction for Lifelong Learning: A Comprehensive Guide to Theory and Practice.* San Francisco: Jossey-Bass, 1991.

Cavaliere, L. A., and Sgroi, A. (eds.). *Learning for Professional Development.* New Directions for Adult and Continuing Education, no. 53. San Francisco: Jossey-Bass, 1992.

Cervero, R. M. *Effective Continuing Education for Professionals.* San Francisco: Jossey-Bass, 1988.

Chi, M.T.H., Glaser, R., and Farr, M. J. (eds.). *The Nature of Expertise.* Hillsdale, N.J.: Erlbaum, 1988.

Clark, M. C. "Transformational Learning." In S. B. Merriam (ed.), *An Update on Adult Learning Theory.* New Directions for Adult and Continuing Education, no. 57. San Francisco: Jossey-Bass, 1993.

Collard, S., and Stalker, J. "Women's Trouble: Women, Gender and the Learning Environment." In R. Hiemstra (ed.), *Creating Environments for Effective Adult Learning.* New Directions for Adult and Continuing Education, no. 50. San Francisco: Jossey-Bass, 1991.

Daloz, L. A. *Effective Teaching and Mentoring: Realizing the Transformational Power of Adult-Learning Experiences.* San Francisco: Jossey-Bass, 1986.

Endorf, M., and McNeff, M. "The Adult Learner: Five Types." *Adult Learning,* 1991, 2 (7), 20–22, 25.

Galbraith, M. W. (ed.). *Adult Learning Methods.* Malabar, Fla.: Krieger, 1990.

Glaser, R. "Thought on Expertise." In C. Schooler and K. Schaie (eds.), *Cognitive Functioning and Social Structure over the Life Course.* Norwood, N.J.: Ablex, 1987.

Hart, A. W. "Effective Administration Through Reflection." *Education and Urban Society,* 1990, 22, 153–169.

Hart, M. V. *Working and Educating for Life.* London: Row Hedge, 1992.

Hayes, E. "Thoughts from Women's Experiences for Teaching and Learning." In E. Hayes (ed.), *Effective Teaching Styles.* New Directions for Continuing Education, no. 43. San Francisco: Jossey-Bass, 1989.

Hiemstra, R. (ed.) *Creating Environments for Effective Adult Learning.* New Directions for Adult and Continuing Education, no. 50. San Francisco: Jossey-Bass, 1991.

Hiemstra, R., and Sisco, B. *Individualizing Instruction: Making Learning Personal, Empowering, and Successful.* San Francisco: Jossey-Bass, 1990.

James, W. B., and Blank, W. E. "Review and Critique of Available Learning Style Inventories." In D. D. Flannery (ed.), *Applying Cognitive Learning Theory to Adult Learning.* New Directions for Adult and Continuing Education, no. 59. San Francisco: Jossey-Bass, 1993.

Jarvis, P. *Adult Learning in the Social Context.* London: Croom Helm, 1987.

Jarvis, P. *Paradoxes of Learning: On Becoming an Individual in Society.* San Francisco: Jossey-Bass, 1992.

Kidd, J. R. *How Adults Learn.* New York: Association Press, 1973.

Kincheloe, J. L., and Steinberg, S. R. "A Tentative Description of Post-Formal Thinking: The Critical Confrontation with Cognitive Theory." *Harvard Educational Review,* 1993, 63 (3), 296–319.

Knowles, M. S. *Self-Directed Learning.* New York: Association Press, 1975.

Knowles, M. S. *The Modern Practice of Adult Education: From Pedagogy to Andragogy.* (2nd ed.) New York: Cambridge Book Company, 1980.

Kolb, D. A. *Experiential Learning: Experience as the Source of Learning and Development.* Englewood Cliffs, N.J.: Prentice Hall, 1984.

Labouvie-Vief, G. "Models of Cognitive Functioning in the Older Adult: Research Needs in Educational Gerontology." In R. H. Sherron and D. B. Lumsden (eds.), *Introduction to Gerontology.* (3rd ed.) New York: Hemisphere, 1990.

Loughlin, K. A., and Mott, V. W. "Models of Women's Learning." In H.K.M. Baskett and V. J. Marsick (eds.), *Professionals' Ways of Knowing: New Findings on How to Improve Professional Education.* New Directions for Adult and Continuing Education, no. 55. San Francisco: Jossey-Bass, 1992.

McCormick, D. W. "The Painful Emotions of Prior Experiential Learning Assessment." *Adult Learning,* 1990, 2 (2), 26–28.

Merriam, S. B. "Adult Learning: Where Have We Come From? Where Are We Headed?" In S. B. Merriam (ed.), *An Update on Adult Learning Theory.* New Directions for Adult and Continuing Education, no. 57. San Francisco: Jossey-Bass, 1993a.

Merriam, S. B. (ed.). *An Update on Adult Learning Theory.* New Directions for Adult and Continuing Education, no. 57. San Francisco: Jossey-Bass, 1993b.

Merriam, S. B., and Caffarella, R. S. *Learning in Adulthood: A Comprehensive Guide.* San Francisco: Jossey-Bass, 1991.

Mezirow, J. *Transformative Dimensions of Adult Learning.* San Francisco: Jossey-Bass, 1991.

Mezirow, J., and Associates. *Fostering Critical Reflection in Adulthood: A Guide to Transformative and Emancipatory Education.* San Francisco: Jossey-Bass, 1990.

Osterman, N. F., and Kottkamp, R. B. *Reflective Practice for Educators.* Newbury Park, Calif.: Corwin Press, 1993.

Pressley, M., Harris, K. R., and Marks, M. B. "But Good Strategy Instructors Are Constructivists!!" *Educational Psychology Review,* in press.

"Promoting Reflection to Improve Practice." *Journal of Staff Development,* 1994, 5 (1), 2–44.

Riegel, K. F. "Dialectic Operations: The Final Period of Cognitive Development." *Human Development,* 1973, *16,* 346–370.

Rybash, J. M., Hoyer, W. J., and Roodin, P. A. *Adult Cognition and Aging.* New York: Pergamon, 1986.

Schneidewind, N. "Feminist Values: Guidelines for Teaching Methodology in Women's Studies." In C. Bunch and S. Pollack (eds.), *Learning Our Way: Essays in Feminist Education.* Freedom, Calif.: Crossing Press, 1983.

Schön, D. A. *The Reflective Practitioner.* New York: Basic Books, 1983.

Schön, D. A. (ed.). *The Reflective Turn.* New York: Teachers College Press, 1991.

Short, P. M., and Rinehart, J. S. "Reflection as a Means of Developing Expertise." *Educational Administrator Quarterly,* 1993, *29* (4), 501–521.

Shrewsbury, C. M. "What is Feminist Pedagogy?" *Women's Studies Quarterly,* 1987, *15* (3), 6–14.

Shuell, T. J. "Cognitive Conceptions of Learning." *Review of Educational Research,* 1986, *56,* 411–436.

Silberman, M. *Active Training.* San Diego: University Associates and Lexington, Mass.: Lexington Books, 1990.

Smith, K. E., and McCormick, D. M. "Translating Experience into Learning: Facilitating the Process for Adult Students." *Adult Learning,* 1992, *3* (5), 22–25.

Stubblefield, H. W., and Keene, P. "The History of Adult Education." In S. B. Merriam and P. M. Cunningham (eds.), *Handbook of Adult and Continuing Education.* San Francisco: Jossey-Bass, 1989.

Tisdell, E. J. "Feminism and Adult Learning: Power, Pedagogy, and Praxis." In S. B. Merriam (ed.), *An Update on Adult Learning Theory.* New Directions for Adult and Continuing Education, no. 57. San Francisco: Jossey-Bass, 1993.

Tremmel, R. "Zen and the Art of Reflective Practice in Teacher Education." *Harvard Educational Review,* 1993, *63* (4), 434–458.

Welton, M. R. "The Contributions of Critical Theory to Our Understanding of Adult Learning." In S. B. Merriam (ed.), *An Update on Adult Learning Theory.* New Directions for Adult and Continuing Education, no. 57. San Francisco: Jossey-Bass, 1993.

Wilson, A. L. "The Promise of Situated Cognition." In S. B. Merriam (ed.), *An Update on Adult Learning Theory.* New Directions for Adult and Continuing Education, no. 57. San Francisco: Jossey-Bass, 1993.

ROSEMARY S. CAFFARELLA is professor in the Division of Educational Leadership and Policy Studies at the University of Northern Colorado.

BRUCE G. BARNETT is associate professor in the Division of Educational Leadership and Policy Studies at the University of Northern Colorado.

Instructional methods and techniques that are consistent with the tenets of experiential learning and that can be used at in-class or field-based sites are described.

Methods and Techniques for Engaging Learners in Experiential Learning Activities

Patty Lee, Rosemary S. Caffarella

In Chapter Three, Caffarella and Barnett examined how considering conjointly the characteristics and needs of adult learners and the conceptual foundations of experiential learning can establish a necessary framework for selecting and coordinating learning activities and assessment procedures that are consistent with experiential learning values and beliefs. In this chapter, we examine specific design and application issues associated with employing experiential learning techniques in the education of adult learners. We first highlight three guideposts to use in the selection and use of experiential learning methods and techniques. We then focus on the "nuts and bolts" of how to use simple instructional techniques for fostering and enhancing the process of experiential learning within the framework of in-class and field-based learning activities and events. We conclude with a discussion of the importance of coordinating and balancing in-class and field-based experiential learning opportunities within learning programs for adults.

Guideposts for Experiential Instructional Activities

Three important guideposts for selecting and using experiential learning methods and techniques in educational programs for adults are drawn from a synthesis of issues raised in the first three chapters of this volume. The first guidepost is that experiential learning methods and procedures are a way of *connecting* each learner's existing knowledge, beliefs, affective characteristics, and experiences with a new set of knowledge, skills, beliefs, and attitudes. This idea is referred to as *knowledge synthesis* and is encapsulated in a definition of learning offered over a decade ago by Goldstein (1978), in which he proposes that learning is a process characterized by "an *expansion* of the knowledge and capacities of the learner in specified ways" (p. 86, italics ours). This definition reinforces the view that the learning of any material, no matter how obtuse or specialized it is, involves a synthesis of preexisting knowledge with newly presented information, and that the learning of this new information is never in isolation from the unique experiential base each learner brings to the instructional situation. A significant implication of this perspective is that educators of adults must be careful not to standardize instructional activities, using the notion that standardization can promote "uniform quality" in learning outcomes. Rather, since standardization leaves out of the learning equation the contributions of each unique learner, it is a misconception to believe that standardization can by itself promote more effective and efficient programs for adults.

The second guidepost is that, in contrast to more traditional approaches to instruction, experiential learning involves a shift in the power base between instructor and learners such that the learners assume more of the responsibility for what is learned and how learning occurs. This shift in learner control is the heart of what *self-directed learning* is all about. Candy (1991) describes four dimensions of self-directed learning that help elucidate this concept: (1) recognizing and fostering personal autonomy, which includes valuing learners as independent agents and guiding their learning by facilitating self-reflection and self-evaluation; (2) supporting self-management in learning, which reinforces the view that adult learners can and should be held accountable for defining the processes and products of their own educational experiences; (3) enhancing learner-control of instruction, which addresses ways in which formal educational programs can empower learners; and (4) collaboratively assisting adult learners in their lifelong pursuit of learning, which reinforces the view that learning is an ongoing and self-sustaining process in which specific formal programs play only a partial role. Taken together, these four dimensions capture the intellectual, philosophical, intuitive, and practical properties of self-directed learning as a cornerstone in the design of instructional activities that are consistent with experiential learning beliefs.

The third and final guidepost is that the transfer of learning from an instructional context (for example, a classroom or workshop experience) to an application context (for example, a job site if training involves new job skills, or completing a job application if training involves literacy) can be enhanced by controlling two properties of the instructional context: (1) the degree of similarity between the instructional contexts and the relevant application contexts, and (2) the depth, elaborateness and comprehensiveness of the skills and information provided in an educational activity or program. These two properties, respectively referred to as *simulation potential* and *knowledge richness,* are not correlated with each other. That is, promoting one property in the learning situation does not invariably result in the promotion of the other property. For example, a person training to be an airline pilot can experience task simulations that closely approximate real flying conditions without experiencing the range and depth of flight conditions and situations that are required to be a successful pilot. Inversely, the pilot trainee can be provided with a wealth of information on the range of atmospheric, mechanical, and human conditions that might be encountered in flight but not in a manner that, in the experiential sense, approximates real-world flight conditions. In the design of methods and techniques for engaging learners, the enhancement of both of these conditions is necessary for the successful transfer of skills, knowledge, and values to real-world situations. In the remaining sections of this chapter, as we describe sample instructional techniques and methods that are experiential in nature, and ways to balance and integrate in-class and field-based learning experiences, we take to account the major components of each of these important guideposts.

Design of In-Class Experiences

In-class experiences can be defined as those activities that are either conducted directly in a "classroom environment," such as college classes, workshops, and conferences, or are performed by learners outside of the learning activity to fulfill program requirements and expectations, such as keeping a journal or practicing specific skills at a work site. In-class activities can facilitate the synthesis between background knowledge and new knowledge to the extent that the activities encourage active reflection or problem solving, especially if they are highly interactive.

In general, learner self-direction can be enhanced by tailoring aspects of a program's content and processes to the identified needs of the learners and ensuring that at least part of the learning activities are grounded in the learners' experiences. This can be done by offering choices in the types of activities and assignments that are to be completed by learners, and by permitting both the flow of the learning events and the amount of time spent on particular issues to vary according to expressed learner needs. However, our experiences with offering learners choice and flexibility indicate that it can be difficult to achieve a balance between instructor control of activities in the interest of fulfilling program goals and objectives and learner control of the content and flow of activities in the interest of meeting personal learning needs.

If there is an especially significant weakness associated with in-class experiences, it is the problem of transferring learning to real-world application situations. Whether it is an educational program for retooling adult learners who are reentering the work force, or a workshop designed to enhance acceptance of ethnic diversity, achieving an adequate degree of simulation between the in-class setting and other real-world settings can be a significant dilemma. On the other hand, knowledge richness in relation to in-class experiences can be substantially enhanced by appropriate experiential learning activities that can contribute to the transfer of learning to real-world contexts.

Table 4.1 defines a number of in-class group methods and techniques for engaging learners in experiential learning. We have included in this table some

Table 4.1. Methods and Techniques for Engaging Learners in Experiential Learning: In-Class Activities

Instructional Methods and Techniques	Description	Suggestions for Enhancing the Learning Experience
Group discussion	A group of five to twenty people have a relatively unstructured exchange of ideas about a specific problem or issue.	Knowledge richness is enhanced when the leader or instructor guides the discussion through a series of iterations that (1) involve variations in the problem or issue, or (2) present the changing implications of different solutions, if the subject matter is a particular problem.
		Learner synthesis of the information can be enhanced by encouraging all members of the class to participate and by directing participants to relate the information to their own experiences.
Reaction panel	A panel of three or four participants reacts to a presentation by an individual or group.	When the presentation addresses issues that have opposing platforms, knowledge richness is enhanced by panels that are composed of members with opposing views or that are directed to present diverse views in their reactions.
		When the presentation addresses specific real-world problems and potential solutions, knowledge richness is enhanced if panels are directed to envision the different futures that would evolve given different solutions.
Listening group	In groups, participants are asked to listen to and observe an assigned part of a speech, panel, or the like.	Knowledge richness is enhanced by using heterogeneous groups that include novices who are directed to ask questions as part of their assigned roles. This provides persons with relatively more expertise opportunities to expound on, and sometimes revise, their own knowledge while enhancing the understanding of the novices.
Demonstration with a return demonstration	A resource person performs an operation or a job, showing others how to do a specified task. Participants are then asked to perform the task that was demonstrated.	Simulation potential is enhanced when class participants go to real-world sites for the demonstrations.
		Self-directed learning is enhanced when participants are involved in the selection of demonstration sites and in the planning of the agenda.

In-class case study	Written or oral presentation of an event, incident, or situation for a small group to analyze and solve.	Self-directed learning and knowledge synthesis are enhanced when the case studies are developed by the participants themselves based on their past or current experiences.
		Follow-up exercises (for example, implementation of a presented solution to a new case) can enhance knowledge synthesis.
		Knowledge richness is enhanced if a case study is followed by an exercise in which persons who must use solutions derived from the case study are expected to intermittently report back to the group on their progress and the results of their activities.
Games	Activities characterized by structured competition or cooperation to provide participants with opportunities to practice specific skills and actions, such as decision making.	Simulation potential is enhanced if persons who typically work or socialize together are teamed together for the games.
		Combining this activity with a reaction panel responsible for observing the players and the course of the game can enhance knowledge richness by encouraging divergent and critical thinking.
In-basket exercises	In a simulation exercise focusing on the "paper symptoms" of a job, participants respond to material people might have in their in-baskets.	Self-directed learning, knowledge synthesis, and simulation potential are enhanced when tasks are selected by the participants from their own experiences.
Critical incidents	Participants are asked to describe an important incident related to a specific aspect of their lives, which is then used as a base for analysis.	Knowledge synthesis is enhanced if learners are directed to reflect on the relation between a reported critical incident and events in their own lives.
		Knowledge richness is enhanced by using with this exercise several listening groups to examine a critical incident from several predefined perspectives and report back on their reflections and findings. Pressing the participants to continue to generate solutions even after the more obvious ones have been expressed can sometimes lead to new ideas that, while sometimes untested, may have high potential.

Table 4.1. (*continued*)

Instructional Methods and Techniques	Description	Suggestions for Enhancing the Learning Experience
Debate	A presentation of conflicting views by two people or two groups in order to clarify the arguments between them.	Knowledge richness is enhanced when persons are required to argue a point of view that they do not necessarily subscribe to. A follow-up writing exercise can encourage self-reflection, thereby enhancing knowledge synthesis.
Poster presentations	Participants develop poster sessions on a given topic or issue. The sessions are presented concurrently on a prearranged date. Participants alternately monitor their own booths to answer questions and dialogue, and attend the sessions of others.	Self-directed learning is enhanced by the flexibility to select the topic for one's poster presentation and by the freedom to control time and effort spent at other poster presentations.
Storytelling	Participants are asked to tell stories that relate how they feel about a particular event or experience.	The addition of a validation process in which participants support, acknowledge, and applaud each other can foster knowledge synthesis.
Journaling	Learners keep a reflective record that focuses on experiences relevant to the content of the program.	Knowledge synthesis and self-directed learning are naturally enhanced in that learners choose the topical focus for journal entries, then construct their own narrative expansions and elaborations based on prior experiences, learning needs, and personal interests.
Modeling and theory building; metaphor construction	Participants (1) construct a diagram, such as a conceptual map, that interrelates the major conceptual components of an issue or set of practices; (2) propose sets of underlying principles to explain a set of phenomena; or (3) identify descriptive metaphors for phenomena (for example, bricklaying as a metaphor for scientific progress).	Knowledge richness is enhanced if this activity is combined with small-group discussions of the models developed by the individual learners, followed by model sharing with the class as a whole.

Case study research	Learners implement or observe the implementation of particular practices in an applied setting, then systematically record and analyze the results.	Self-directed learning is especially enhanced when a participant has a real-world critical situation or issue that can be examined by means of an intense case study.
		Knowledge richness is enhanced if case studies are shared in class discussions, especially when similar cases are managed in different ways by different participants.
Role assumption exercise	Participants intentionally place themselves in situations or seek experiences that they would not normally engage in (1) to gain understanding of the life experiences of others (for example, volunteering in a prison), or (2) to gain fresh perspectives on their own experiences (for example, adventure programming).	Knowledge synthesis is enhanced by combining this activity with journaling.
Trips and tours	Learners go on a field trip for on-site observation and learning.	Simulation potential is enhanced if trips involve contexts in which the roles, tasks, and values are similar to those associated with the contexts that learners will be expected to perform in; however, these visits might prove counterproductive if values are changing in the field as a whole.
		Knowledge synthesis is enhanced when field trips are followed by in-class discussions that are guided by learners' different reactions to their experiences on the trips.

Source: Adapted from Caffarella (1992), Caffarella (in press), and Jackson and Rosenberg (1990).

suggestions for enhancing each technique's value in relation to knowledge synthesis, self-directed learning, simulation potential, and knowledge richness
(each described earlier in this chapter). Enhancing knowledge richness is especially emphasized in this table.

Design of Field-Based Experiences

Field-based experiences are instructional activities which are conducted
directly in relevant real-world environments, such as internships, on-the-job
training, and apprenticeships. Field-based experiences are "authentic" in the
sense that they provide adult learners with opportunities to use or closely
observe skills, the impact of particular values, and relevant response patterns
within the contexts in which these actions make the most sense. However,
since field-based learning experiences are often associated with particular sites,
are sometimes guided by "masters" who may be set in their ways with respect
to what they accept as best practice, and may require quick decisions that do
not permit extended reflection, they should not be viewed as the most legitimate contexts for learning. There is a place for learning in which learners "step
out" of the real-world situations that, because of habit and pressures to con-
form to tradition, tend to inhibit the kinds of problem solving and active reflection that will produce the "next generation" of ideas and solutions.

Table 4.2 (see p. 52) offers a number of examples and techniques for
delivering experiential learning activities in the field. As in Table 4.1, we have
included in this table suggestions for enhancing a method's value in relation to
knowledge synthesis, self-directed learning, knowledge richness and simulation potential. Note that there is considerable overlap in these delivery methods and techniques; for example, coaching, mentoring, and on-the-job training
can occur in combination.

Coordination of In-Class and Field-Based
Learning Experiences

The intended outcome of a particular configuration of in-class and field-based
learning experiences is learners who can enter more competently into a particular arena of human action, whether it is a job or profession, a set of interpersonal relationships, a leisure pursuit, or a realm of human endeavor such
as poetry or drama. Educators and trainers have often neglected the important
task of attempting to achieve a balance between field-based and in-class experiences that can promote in different learners a readiness for new tasks, roles,
and responsibilities. For example, it is not uncommon to see activities and programs that, adhering to tradition, provide field-based experiences primarily at
the very end of the in-class portion of the program, apparently based on the
idea that learners first gain "theory and understanding" in the classroom and
then follow this with "practical applications."

As indicated by Lewis and Williams (Chapter One), a major tenet of reflective practice is the cyclical nature of action and reflection. As described by Kolb (1984) and his colleagues (cited in Lewis and Williams), it involves periods of concrete experience, reflection, the formation of new ideas and hypotheses, and knowledge testing and application. From this perspective, the relationship between in-class and field-based learning experiences should have more of a leapfrog-like quality. Novice and more capable learners alike could benefit from intermittent field-based experiences followed by classroom experiences, with action and reflection being an integral component in each arena. Also, if the learning process is to be self-directed, we envision more of a mosaic quality to the learning activities: Adult learners work from a menu of choices involving a rich array of potential in-class activities and field-based experiences. Moreover, as illustrated in the next two chapters, assessment activities would be configured to each learner's patterns of knowledge acquisition and growth, rather than being pre-defined as rigid sets of outcomes and standards by which all learners must ultimately be judged.

Such patterns of learning and assessment, although certainly consistent with much that we have known about reflective practice for some time now, fly in the face of the learning activities and programs for adult learners that we often see, whether they are workshops, professional development classes, or community college and university programs. At the very least, the model of experiential learning that we are presenting supports two modest recommendations for the coordination of in-class and field-based learning experiences. First, educational programs for adult learners benefit if more of the instructional experiences are field-based. Second, field experiences should be coupled with ongoing in-class and individually chosen learning activities, both of which combine the presentation of new information with active reflection so that the learner's field-based experiences would increasingly assume new levels of meaning. Within this perspective, personal and professional competence—the ability to perform particular roles or functions—would be acquired as a product of the larger pattern of growth, rather than being conceptualized as the ultimate outcome of a set of educational experiences. In other words, competence ceases to be a rite of initiation and assumes its rightful place as an ongoing reflection of the growth process.

Conclusion

This chapter has identified and examined methods and techniques for engaging adult learners in experiential learning activities, using the process model that is the centerpiece of this work (see Chapter Two) as the basis for discussion. The chapter began by affirming several key points about learning, including the importance of viewing learning as a synthesis of new and existing information, the major role that self-direction plays in the learning process, and the fact that transfer of learning is influenced by both the richness of the

Table 4.2. Methods and Formats for Delivering Experiential Learning Activities in the Field

Method or Technique	Description	Suggestions for Enhancing the Learning Experience
Analysis of practice	Participants examine in real-world contexts how they perform certain activities or roles, or how they react to certain situations.	Knowledge synthesis is enhanced by combining this activity with journaling (see Table 4.1).
		Self-directed learning is enhanced by having learners complete a discrepancy analysis, in which they contrast their current practices with what they believe they should be doing.
		Knowledge richness is enhanced by having learners prepare checklists of the different types of responses that a job, a social situation, or a critical incident requires of a person.
Apprenticeship	Formal relationship between employer and employee through which an employee is trained for a craft or skill through practical experience under the supervision of experienced workers.	Knowledge synthesis is enhanced by combining apprenticeships with journaling (see Table 4.1).
		Knowledge richness is enhanced by combining field experiences with in-class group discussion (see Table 4.1).
Coaching	One-to-one learning by demonstration and practice, with immediate feedback, which usually is conducted by peers, supervisors, or experts in the field.	Self-directed learning is enhanced when coaches leave latitude for learners to make mistakes, then assist them in reflecting on their actions and choosing a new course of action for future encounters with similar situations.
Internship or practicum	Learning through supervised, practical experience within one or more relevant real-world settings. Supervision can be managed in several ways, including full mentoring relationship (see next entry) or intermittent conferences with one or more supervising experts.	A wrap-up experience with an in-class reaction panel (see Table 4.1) can enhance knowledge synthesis and knowledge richness.
Mentoring	Involves an intense caring relationship in which persons with more experience work with specific learners to promote professional and personal growth. Mentors model expected behavior and values and provide support and a sounding board for their protégés.	Because of its emphasis on emotional support, mentoring may be especially useful when the required skills and values are substantially different from those already in the learner's repertoire. In other words, mentoring may facilitate knowledge synthesis when the to-be-learned material is difficult or very new to the learner.

Clinical Supervision	A collegial practice designed to support and give feedback to learners who generally are already good at what they do. The process consists of five steps (pre-observation conference, observation and data collection, analysis and strategy session, follow-up conference, and postconference analysis), which are used to refine practice.	At least with respect to job training, knowledge richness is enhanced when clinical supervision, performed by a person associated with the formal learning program, is combined with mentoring, performed by a second person who is closer to the specific job site. This dual relationship ensures that learners experiencing clinical supervision are receiving multiple perspectives on their task performance and problem-solving skills.
On-the-job training	A master or expert worker provides instruction to the novice while both are engaged in productive work on the job. Often used when work is complex and the worker or craft person is the best person to pass on knowledge and skills to the learner.	Knowledge synthesis and self-directed learning are enhanced if learners have some control over the order of learning experiences that will occur during the course of the training.

Knowledge richness is enhanced if on-the-job training is combined with a series of planned visits to other sites in which similar roles and tasks are performed but in somewhat different ways in comparison to the job site (see Trips and tours in Table 4.1). |
Clinics	Sessions focus on a single problem or skill in which participants present case illustrations of practice problems to an expert or panel of experts. The experts serve in consultant roles.	Self-directed learning is enhanced if learners who are participating in internships or on-the-job training are expected to concurrently participate in clinics in which they are responsible for bringing forward their own unique problems and issues for discussion by the experts.
Support groups	Groups in which people work together on shared problems or practices. Usually participation is voluntary, and sharing and equal status among group members are the norm.	Knowledge synthesis and knowledge richness are enhanced when the formation of "circles of support" is actively encouraged and facilitated by members of the formal program faculty.
People networking	Forming loosely configured groups of people who have similar experiences, interests, problems, or ideas for the purposes of giving and receiving information and providing mutual support and assistance.	Transfer of learning is more likely when networking continues among program participants long after formal program completion. Long-term networking supports a learner's ongoing problem solving and the contributing processes of knowledge synthesis and self-directed learning.

Source: Adapted from Caffarella (1992), Caffarella (in press), and Jackson and Rosenberg (1990).

information being taught and the degree to which instructional settings and activities simulate those in real-world contexts. Consistent with the model, methods and techniques for experiential learning for both in-class and field-based learning experiences were then described. Finally, the coordination of field-based and in-class learning experiences was discussed, emphasizing the importance of using field experiences as a framework for conceptualizing the in-class activities.

The emphasis of this and earlier chapters on learner reflection points out the importance of the feedback process as one key to successful growth and learning. As we know from cognition research (Neisser and Harsch, 1992), reflection is subject to the same kinds of memory errors that are present in other forms of information retention. In the next chapter, Barnett and Lee expound on the ways authentic assessment procedures, which entail the documentation of change, can become routine parts of educational programs for adults that embrace the precepts of experiential learning.

References

Caffarella, R. S. *Psychosocial Development of Women: Linkages to the Practice of Teaching and Learning in Adult Education.* Columbus, Ohio: ERIC Clearinghouse on Adult, Career and Vocational Education, 1992.

Caffarella, R. S. *Planning Programs for Adult Learners: A Practical Guide for Educators, Trainers, and Staff Developers.* San Francisco: Jossey-Bass, in press.

Candy, P. C. *Self-Direction for Lifelong Learning: A Comprehensive Guide to Theory and Practice.* San Francisco: Jossey-Bass, 1991.

Goldstein, M. B. "Achieving the Nondiscriminatory Recognition of Experiential Learning." In M. T. Keeton and P. J. Tate (eds.), *Learning by Experience: What, Why, and How.* New Directions for Experiential Learning, no. 1. San Francisco: Jossey-Bass, 1978.

Jackson, L. B., and Rosenberg, M. "Planning Effective Practicum Experiences in Regular Schools for Nontraditional Teacher Trainees." Annual conference of the Teacher Education Division of the Council for Exceptional Children, Anchorage, Alaska, Nov. 1990.

Kolb, D. A. *Experiential Learning and Development.* Englewood Cliffs, N.J.: Prentice Hall, 1984.

Neisser, U., and Harsch, N. "Phantom Flashbulbs: False Recollections of Hearing the News of *Challenger.*" In E. Winograd and U. Neisser (eds.), *Affect and Accuracy in Recall: Studies of "Flashbulb" Memories.* Cambridge, England: Cambridge University Press, 1992.

PATTY LEE is assistant professor in the Division of Special Education at the University of Northern Colorado.

ROSEMARY S. CAFFARELLA is professor in the Division of Educational Leadership and Policy Studies at the University of Northern Colorado.

The creation of a portfolio documenting adults' experiences is gaining acceptance in higher education as well as in business and industry. We describe a critical first step in portfolio construction—the development of a folio of relevant materials documenting a person's learning.

Assessment Processes and Outcomes: Building a Folio

Bruce G. Barnett, Patty Lee

Accurately capturing what adults are learning and how their thinking has changed is a challenge for adult educators, whether in higher education, corporate, or other settings in which learning programs for adults occur. To merely document with transcripts or certificates of achievement the courses, seminars, or workshops learners have successfully completed ignores the importance these experiences have on their growth and development. Besides recording the occurrence of these events, adult educators need to assist learners in determining the meaning or relevancy they are deriving from these formal learning experiences.

Portfolios are being touted as a productive way to capture what adults are learning as well as the personal meaning they attach to these experiences. The actual creation of a portfolio will be examined in the next chapter; however, in this chapter, we examine the initial step in portfolio construction, namely the development of a *folio* that is a compilation of the products, materials, and activities adults accumulate as a result of their learning experiences. We begin our discussion of folios by addressing the importance of obtaining "authentic" measures of learners' real-life performances. Two different types of materials that can be included in a folio—artifacts and attestations—are then described. We conclude by suggesting important issues adult educators must consider when assisting learners in developing their folios.

Authentic Assessment

Formally assessing the skills and knowledge adults gain as they participate in various experiential learning activities in such settings as higher education, business and industry, and literacy programs can be a labor-intensive task. Typically, standardized tests, observations of performance, or checklists have been used to assess adults' learning experiences and capabilities. Unfortunately, these tools may not capture the true essence of what has been learned or how learning has evolved. Therefore, a growing number of educators are recommending that *authentic assessment* measures be used to ascertain children's as well as adults' learning (Wiggins, 1989; Case, 1992). The use of authentic assessment is particularly relevant when determining adults' experiential learning because " . . . *authentic assessment* refers to measuring the real, actual, or genuine [experience] as opposed to measuring a poor substitute" (Case, 1992, p. 19, italics in original). As such, learners are allowed to apply their knowledge by showing what they know and can do.

The calls for authentic assessment are particularly relevant for measuring adults' experiential learning. For instance, there is increasing pressure on higher education institutions to become more accountable for undergraduate and graduate students' learning, especially as this learning translates to the workplace. Therefore, more "active" learning activities are being utilized within and outside college classrooms. Problem-based learning, role plays, simulations, "in-basket" exercises, critical incidents, and socio-drama are all designed to actively engage adults in the learning process. Likewise, field-based learning, as evidenced by practicums, internships, and service learning activities, are becoming more prominent.

Furthermore, in business and industry settings, employees are being asked to actively engage in solving persistent problems and in assessing corporate needs. This trend is clearly illustrated by the examples of action learning, Future Search, and outdoor education that Lewis and Williams provide in Chapter One. As a result of these workplace activities, adults are accumulating additional meaningful and authentic experiences which can be assessed.

If authentic assessment is becoming a viable way to measure adult learning, what forms might this assessment take? Roland Case (1992) suggests three types of authentic assessment: *Performance assessment* is the person's ability to use ideas either by completing a complex task (for example, performing a dramatic piece, conducting an experiment) or by producing an object (for example, designing a building, making a film).

Naturalistic assessment occurs when someone else gathers information about a person's normal work activities by observing his or her performance, gathering documents, or talking to other people about the person's accomplishments. *Portfolio assessment* consists of individuals compiling a collection of materials documenting their learning experiences over a substantial length of time.

These forms of assessment are not mutually exclusive. Although each form of authentic assessment has merit in obtaining realistic and genuine information about adults' learning experiences, portfolio assessment can and should encompass both performance and naturalistic assessment. Although recent attention has been directed at the appropriateness of portfolios for students in K-12 school settings (Johnson, 1992), there is a rich history of portfolio use in adult education. For instance, as an acceptable alternative to traditional teacher assessment procedures, portfolios are being used to capture classroom teachers' performances (Edgerton, Hutching, and Quinlan, 1991; Wolf, 1991). In addition, portfolios have been used in postsecondary education to allow student teachers to capture the complexities of the teaching and learning process, adult students who return to postsecondary education to receive college credit for previous experiences, and graduate students to assess the learning obtained through formal coursework and field experiences. By assessing the knowledge, skills, and competencies they have gained (as Caffarella and Lee note in Chapter Four), adults focus on their accomplishments rather than on their deficiencies, reflecting their cumulative professional development and the lifelong nature of learning. As these examples illustrate, performance and naturalistic assessment measures are quite appropriate for inclusion in a folio.

Developing a Folio

We will now discuss two issues that must be addressed when assembling a folio: (1) How does a folio differ from a portfolio? and (2) What materials go into a folio?

What Is a Folio? In preparing portfolios, an important distinction is made between the *folio* and the *portfolio*. The portfolio is the finished product that contains only selected documents displaying appropriate evidence of the learner's knowledge, skills, and dispositions (Bird, 1990). A folio, on the other hand, is the accumulation of all possible materials representing a person's learning; it is not a selective set of documents (MacIsaac, 1991).

A folio consists of a large array of products, materials, and other evidence of activities and experiences learners accumulate as they participate in different learning situations. For example, business executives might include evidence of professional degrees and training, corporate investments and earnings, and leadership accomplishments in their folios. A folio constructed while adults participate in a literacy program might include audio tapes of their reading performance, the instructor's written evaluations, and examples of written assignments.

What Types of Evidence Are Included in a Folio? Numerous suggestions exist regarding the types of information that are appropriate to include in a folio (Barba, Carrolton, and Yeaw, 1984; Kemp, Smith, and Van Sant, 1984; Weissman, 1984; MacIsaac, 1991; Wolf, 1991). In considering what to collect and present in a folio, two major types of evidence, which are illustrated in Table 5.1, have been deemed appropriate—artifacts produced or facilitated by the learner and attestations prepared by other people (Bird, 1990; Edgerton, Hutching, and Quinlan, 1991; Barton and Collins, 1993). Using Case's (1992) typology of authentic assessment described above, artifacts are a form of performance assessment while attestations would be considered naturalistic assessment measures. In the remainder of this chapter, we will examine how folios are constructed by providing examples of these two types of folio entries and by identifying several key issues to consider when selecting evidence for the folio.

Table 5.1. Types of Entries Included in Folios

Artifacts (Created or facilitated by learner)	Attestations (Created by other people or organizations)
Written correspondence, memos	Letters of recommendation
Term papers	Letters from parents and clients
Artistic materials: paintings, weavings, pottery	Job performance evaluations
Video/audio tapes of performance	Newspaper and other media accounts
Educational platforms	Honors and awards
Journals, critical incident reports	Community surveys
Resumes, autobiographies	Certificates and licenses
Professional development plans	Diplomas
Published articles, books	Transcripts of college coursework
Students' work, test scores	Test results
Corporate earnings, investments	Records of employment
Budgets and economic forecasts	
Computer programs	

During the normal course of engaging in learning and work-related tasks, adults may create tangible products on their own, or they may be responsible for facilitating the development of products by other people. These products can be included in a folio as *artifacts* (see Table 5.1). A vast array of artifacts may be created individually by the learner. For instance, products and materials may be developed in higher education settings as adult learners participate in formal classroom and field-based learning activities. Course assignments, documents created during in-basket exercises, and position or term papers are particularly appropriate artifacts to include in a folio. Learners might demonstrate their skills and competencies by participating in role plays and simulation activities during class sessions. These events can be documented using audio tapes, observational records, or photographs. Certain in-class events, such as a debate or a mock press conference, are conducive to being videotaped for future review and critique. During field-based learning experiences (such as internships and mentor programs), learners might keep written journals or critical incident reports which document particularly important events, capturing the learner's personal reflection through an in-depth description of the event as well as personal insights gained from the experience.

Artifacts may also be collected as adults engage in their work-related tasks. During their involvement in professional development seminars and workshops, adults may work independently to develop curricular materials, paintings, or video productions. Similarly, products developed on the job, such as resumes, published articles, computer programs, and professional development plans, are valuable artifacts for inclusion in the folio.

An illustration of a particularly useful artifact for people engaged in educational programs (from professional educators to volunteers to board mem-

bers) is an *educational platform* or philosophy statement. In educational platforms, adults articulate their beliefs, values, and aspirations, especially those
that affect the processes and outcomes related to their work or volunteer settings (Kottkamp, 1990; Zinn, 1990; Barnett, 1992; Caffarella, in press).
Instructors and facilitators can assist learners in the types of information to
include in an educational platform. For instance, teachers, learners, and business leaders might state their views about learner outcomes needed to succeed
in today's society; the preferred types of instructional methods and materials
to use in teaching; the leadership behavior required in institutions to develop
a productive learning environment; and the desired relationships between business and industry, educational organizations, and local communities. In addition, Future Search activities (see Lewis and Williams, Chapter One) allow
employees in business and industrial settings to clarify their personal values
and to articulate the desirable future states of their organizations. Not only are
platforms and Future Search materials useful as tangible products to include
in the folio, but they also provide a mechanism for preparing adults to com-
municate their ideals to prospective employers, coworkers, and clientele.

Besides artifacts that learners are solely responsible for creating, it is highly
appropriate to include folio entries that learners facilitate other people to
develop (Bird, 1990; MacIsaac, 1991). Given the recent importance of shared
leadership, site-based management, and participatory decision making, col-
laboratively-developed artifacts may become increasingly popular and relevant
folio entries. Teachers, for example, may wish to include copies of their students' work and test scores as evidence of student progress while under their
direction. Other instances of artifacts resulting from the learner's impact might
include organizational improvement plans, corporate earnings and investments, budgets and economic forecasts, and quarterly and annual reports.

In addition to those artifacts produced or facilitated by the learner, documents prepared by other people, attesting to the learner's worth or capabilities, are also desirable for inclusion in a folio. These *attestations* (see Table 5.1)
can be from supervisors, friends, clients, or coworkers, or they can be documents produced by professional organizations and associations. Bird (1990)
suggests three different types of entries that may be produced by others: informal commentaries, structured attestations, and official records. *Informal commentaries* are nonstructured feedback about the learner's capabilities depicted
in general letters of recommendation and notes from clients or customers.
More formal written responses, including structured observation records, job
performance evaluations, or surveys from community members or clients, are
referred to as *structured attestations*. Finally, learners may obtain *official records*
from colleges and universities, licensure boards, and present and former places
of employment confirming their accomplishments. Examples of these records
are transcripts, diplomas, certificates and licenses, and records of employment.
Regardless of who or what organization provides evidence of a person's accomplishments, these attestations provide useful information in the folio about the
learner's expertise, competence, and skill levels.

Additional Considerations in Folio Construction. Rather than deciding whether artifacts or attestations are the best source of evidence for inclusion in a folio, these types of documents can overlap and complement each other. Artifacts capture the naturally occurring products resulting from learners' experiences while attestations provide outsiders' perspectives about the learners' accomplishments. For instance, while learning how to use computers, learners might document their skills and knowledge in a folio by collecting artifacts such as spreadsheets, computer programs, and journals documenting their progress as well as by obtaining attestations in the form of written feedback from instructors on course assignments, a certificate noting the successful completion of a computer workshop, and a college transcript documenting computer courses they have taken.

Barton and Collins (1993) suggest several additional questions that should be addressed as portfolios are prepared. These considerations also are relevant in the construction of folios:

How much evidence should be included in the folio? Although it may be difficult to know how much information to include, a good rule of thumb is not to be too selective. Because learners may create several versions of a portfolio (see MacIsaac and Jackson, Chapter Six), a substantial number of both artifacts and attestations should be included in the folio. Deciding only to collect a large number of artifacts at the expense of obtaining any attestations may have serious consequences for the learner when organizing materials into the final portfolio.

How should the information be organized? Addressing this question is probably more appropriate as the actual portfolio is created. Nevertheless, sorting evidence into artifacts and attestations is an initial form of organization. This categorization system allows portfolio preparers to determine where they may have too much or too little evidence. By having a wealth of evidence in the folio, learners will have numerous options when deciding how best to organize and display their materials.

Who decides what to include in the folio? An underlying assumption of portfolio construction is that learners are self-directed and are therefore the best judges of what artifacts and attestations to incorporate in their folios. This presumes learners are knowledgeable about authentic assessment and are capable of making informed decisions regarding the types of evidence to collect. Novice portfolio developers, however, will probably need guidance and assistance from an instructor or facilitator. Suggestions from an instructor who is experienced in portfolio construction are not meant to dictate what evidence to collect; rather they are intended to enhance the quality and variety of evidence being collected. For instance, adults with little experience in portfolio construction may only include written documents and ignore other types of evidence such as photographs of final products, videotapes of performance, or the actual products themselves (for example, pottery, paintings, clothing).

It is apparent that no one piece or type of evidence is most suitable for inclusion in a folio. Learners, who are ultimately responsible for folio composition, must give careful attention to obtaining evidence which is credible and accurately reflects their authentic learning experiences. Folios, therefore, should be extensive and, as we have pointed out, should incorporate both performance and naturalistic assessment measures. Without a wide array of quality folio entries, learners will be hindered when selecting final entries for their portfolio from this compilation of materials. The well-stocked folio increases the likelihood of learners producing portfolios that not only document the breadth of their experiences, but also represent the depth of their understanding.

Conclusion

In this chapter we have examined a range of assessment procedures that can provide comprehensive and authentic measures of growth and change in adult learners as they participate in formal educational programs and engage in their work-related tasks. The focus has been on how learners can employ both naturalistic and performance assessment measures when constructing a folio consisting of learner-produced artifacts and non-learner–produced attestations. Folios then provide the basis for portfolio construction, which is the topic of the next chapter by MacIsaac and Jackson.

References

Barba, M. P., Carrolton, E. T., and Yeaw, E.M.J. "Portfolio Assessment of the RN Student." Paper presented at the annual National Conference on Non-traditional and Interdisciplinary Programs, Arlington, Va., 1984.

Barnett, B. G. "Using Alternative Assessment Measures in Educational Leadership Preparation Programs: Educational Platforms and Portfolios." *Journal of Personnel Evaluation in Education,* 1992, 6, 141–151.

Barton, J., and Collins, A. "Portfolios in Teacher Education." *Journal of Teacher Education,* 1993, 44 (3), 200–210.

Bird, T. "The Schoolteacher's Portfolio: An Essay on Possibilities." In J. Millman and L. Darling-Hammond (eds.), *The New Handbook of Teacher Evaluation: Assessing Elementary and Secondary Personnel.* (2nd ed.) Newbury Park, Calif.: Corwin Press, 1990.

Caffarella, R. S. *Planning Programs for Adult Learners: A Practical Guide for Educators, Trainers, and Staff Developers.* San Francisco: Jossey-Bass, in press.

Case, R. "On the Need to Assess Authentically." *Holistic Education Review,* 1992, 5 (4), 14–23.

Edgerton, R., Hutching, P., and Quinlan, K. *The Teaching Portfolio: Capturing the Scholarship in Teaching.* Washington, D.C.: American Association for Higher Education, 1991.

Johnson, B. "Creating Performance Assessments." *Holistic Education Review,* 1992, 5 (4), 38–44.

Kemp, W., Smith, R., and Van Sant, G. "Evaluating Experiential Learning: The Portfolio." Paper presented at the annual National Conference on Non-traditional and Interdisciplinary Programs, Arlington, Va., 1984.

Kottkamp, R. "The Administrative Platform as a Means of Reflection: A Ten Year Assessment." Paper presented at the annual meeting of the American Educational Research Association, Boston, 1990.

MacIsaac, D. "Teacher Induction Partnerships: Portfolio Development Guide." Greeley, Colo.: University of Northern Colorado, 1991.

Weissman, K. T. "Evaluating Life-experience Credits for Working Adult Students in an Accelerated Off-campus Program." Paper presented at the annual National Conference on Non-traditional and Interdisciplinary Programs, Arlington, Va., 1984.

Wiggins, G. "A True Test: Toward More Authentic and Equitable Assessment." *Phi Delta Kappan,* 1989, *70* (9), 703–715.

Wolf, K. "The Schoolteacher's Portfolio: Issues in Design, Implementation, and Evaluation." *Phi Delta Kappan,* 1991, *73* (2), 129–136.

Zinn, L. M. "Identifying Your Philosophical Orientation." In M. W. Galbraith (ed.), *Adult Learning Methods.* Malabar, Fla.: Krieger, 1990.

BRUCE G. BARNETT is associate professor in the Division of Educational Leadership and Policy Studies at the University of Northern Colorado.

PATTY LEE is assistant professor in the Division of Special Education at the University of Northern Colorado.

*This chapter defines and discusses the concept of the portfolio in
terms of its essential features, then examines the various functions
that portfolios serve in the assessment of adult learning and the role
that portfolios play in reflective processes.*

Assessment Processes and Outcomes: Portfolio Construction

Doug MacIsaac, Lewis Jackson

The use of portfolios is a time-honored and respected convention within a variety of professions. Artists, photographers, architects, and designers are among those who routinely employ portfolios as one way of representing the range and quality of their work. Portfolios are also utilized as an assessment of prior learning for college credit and as a measure of learners' personal accomplishments in fields such as business, law, and medicine (Geiger and Shugarman, 1988). In education, portfolios have gained currency as a more authentic approach for assessing student learning at the elementary, middle, and secondary school level (Hansen, 1992; Knight, 1992; Wolf, 1989) and, increasingly, school systems are beginning to develop the portfolio as a district-wide assessment tool (Matthews, 1990). In addition, portfolios are being used with greater frequency with adult learners in a variety of settings. For example, portfolio development is being incorporated into undergraduate and graduate programs, in business and industry, in new teacher induction programs, and as a form of faculty development in schools and colleges.

As an assessment technique, portfolios have been characterized as an alternative form of assessment that promotes the development of self-assessment skills in learners (Tierney, Carter, and Desai, 1991; Arter and Spandel, 1992). Barnett (1992) suggests that portfolios are "a viable means for documenting a learner's performance, revealing his/her accumulated knowledge and skills" (p. 142). Strengths frequently associated with portfolio use include: "learners share in the responsibility for assessing their work, data are gathered and evaluated continuously over the course of the learning project (versus only at the end of the activity), learners have the opportunity to learn about their own learning, and learners and other stakeholders develop an expanded view of what is learned" (ERIC, 1993, p. 1).

NEW DIRECTIONS FOR ADULT AND CONTINUING EDUCATION, no. 62, Summer 1994 © Jossey-Bass Inc., Publishers

In the preceding chapter, Barnett and Lee draw a distinction between a folio and a portfolio in the documentation of adult learning activities. Whereas the folio represents the larger collection of a learner's work, the portfolio is a subset of the folio materials that has been specifically selected for a particular purpose. In other words, a portfolio is a carefully edited and tailored collection of artifacts and attestations that are selected from the folio that documents an individual's learning and accomplishments over time. We begin this chapter with a discussion of the characteristics of a portfolio, starting with a working definition of a learning portfolio and followed by an elaboration of specific features of this definition. Explained in the next section are the varied purposes and functions that a portfolio might serve, including self-assessment and self-reflection, assessing a learners' progress in a program, and self-presentation to external sources. The chapter concludes with a discussion of the importance of learner reflection with respect to the construction and use of portfolios.

A Working Definition

Exactly what is a portfolio? At present, there is much discussion regarding this query and, seemingly, much latitude for inventive interpretation (Hutchings, 1990; Graves and Sunstein, 1992; O'Neil, 1993). In a general sense, a portfolio is a purposeful collection of a learner's work assembled over time that documents one's efforts, progress, and achievements (Arter and Spandel, 1992). In addition, a portfolio "embodies an attitude that assessment is dynamic and that the richest portrayals of . . . performance are based on multiple sources of evidence collected over time in authentic settings" (Wolf, 1991). Borrowing from the work of Kenneth Wolf on the construction and assessment of teaching portfolios (Wolf, personal communication, August 1993), a portfolio is defined as the structured documented history of a carefully selected assembly of coached or mentored accomplishments substantiated by materials (artifacts and attestations) that represent a learner's work. These materials are accompanied by descriptive explanations and commentaries in which the learner defines, describes, and reflects on the accomplishments represented in the portfolio. Discussed in the following subsections are the distinctive features of a portfolio derived from this definition.

The Portfolio as a Documented History of Learning. A portfolio is more than a written account of one's accomplishments. Portfolios need to provide direct evidence of learning, and this is accomplished through the careful selection of materials. Not only are such materials critical for assessing the nature of learners' capabilities and competencies, they are also a valuable vehicle for fostering focused and meaningful conversations between learners and instructors (Hutchings, 1990). A major advantage of portfolios over other forms of assessment is that portfolios provide the opportunity to view learning as it occurs across time, allowing for the processes as well as the products of one's learning to become visible. Take, for example, Buttra, a Cambodian who lived in Galang, a South East Asian refugee camp located in Indonesia.

Over the four-year period that Buttra waited to be accepted for resettlement in the United States, he was employed by several human service agencies in a variety of work roles. Prior to resettlement in the United States, Buttra received intensive training in English, cultural orientation, and pre-employment skills. During the course of training Buttra served as classroom translator and teacher's aide. One of the goals of the cultural orientation process was to translate skills and knowledge that are functional within a traditional society for export into the American workplace through the development of a personal portfolio. When Buttra departed Galang for the United States, he carried with him a portfolio consisting of a letter of introduction to prospective employers, a résumé documenting his work experience in Cambodia as well as Galang, letters of recommendation from supervisors and teachers, and a diploma acknowledging the completion of the training program. Buttra's portfolio, as a documentation of both prior knowledge and skills and newly acquired knowledge and skills, served as a measure of occupational readiness with which he could promote himself to prospective employers.

The Portfolio as a Structured and Selective Record of Accomplishments. To what extent should a portfolio be structured is a much debated topic. Although learners should be permitted great flexibility in constructing their portfolios so that their unique voices are heard, the portfolio process and its products must be configured in a manner that enhances the way information is communicated to portfolio users. Structuring the portfolio entails broadly specifying documentation criteria to ensure that learners provide specific types of evidence recognized as essential indicators of effectiveness and competence. For example, when using portfolios to assess prior learning in higher education programs serving adult learners, where the focus is on identifying competencies already acquired, learners should include within their portfolios material that both substantiates and verifies prior learning as well as clearly demonstrates the level of competence for which the advanced standing is sought. Letters from employers, transcripts of workshops or courses completed, videotapes demonstrating on-the-job performance, certificates acknowledging the successful completion of training programs, and official reports indicating credit earned by examination are examples of the material that such a portfolio would likely contain.

To prevent the portfolio from becoming "a thick and unwieldy collection of documents and materials," the portfolio should contain a critical set of accomplishments, rather than the totality of learners' activities and experiences (Wolf, 1991, p. 131). That is, as also noted by Barnett and Lee in Chapter Five, a portfolio should contain carefully selected materials as opposed to every project and activity that the learner has engaged in. For example, Maria, an autoworker in Detroit, has just completed a company-sponsored retraining program. Major components of this program included training in the areas of literacy, mathematical computation, and statistical process control. Throughout her training, Maria completed a series of individual learning modules, participated in workshops focusing on total quality management, and responded in writing to work-related vignettes that required her to apply her knowledge of statistical process control and total quality management. Maria opted to include in her portfolio assessment scores for the modules she completed; a videotape of her participation in quality learning circles; edited vignettes that demonstrate such areas as problem-solving skills and her ability to apply statistical process control techniques to work-related situations; a certificate indicating successful completion of the training program; and finally, a letter of recommendation from her supervisor. As Maria applies for newly created positions within the company, her portfolio will be reviewed as one component of the interviewing process.

Structuring the portfolio serves several purposes. First, an identified structure reduces the amount of guesswork on the part of learners regarding the documentation process, thereby increasing the likelihood that relevant materials will be included. Second, structuring the portfolio also helps to ensure that the portfolio contains a full range of information with regard to those areas recognized as central to a given purpose for constructing the portfolio. Third, a focused approach to portfolio construction minimizes concerns of manageability and maximizes the probability that the portfolio will hold meaning for both the creator and the consumer. Finally, structuring the portfolio around key dimensions of performance not only directs learners to the most important documentation tasks, but also provides a common focus which creates the opportunity for learners to work together on their portfolios as well as their learning.

The Portfolio as a Collaborative Process. Constructing a portfolio should not be considered a solo performance, but a collaborative one (Shulman, 1988; Wolf, 1991). Collaboration with other learners, colleagues, and instructors through supportive coaching or mentoring is considered by many to be one of the portfolio's greatest strengths (Elbow and Belanoff, 1986; Shulman, 1988; Bird, 1990; Hutchings, 1990; Wolf, 1991). In support of a collaborative approach to portfolio construction, Seldin (1991) has observed:

> Some may argue that the portfolio contents will be colored by second-party assistance and therefore is less useful because it represents "coached" performance. But Shulman (1988) disposes with this objection by arguing that portfolio development *should* involve interaction and mentoring in the same way that a doctoral dissertation reflects both the efforts of the candidate and the advice of the advisor. The solution to the so-called problem of coaching, he says, is to turn it around and treat it as a virtue. [p. 5]

A portfolio constructed in the company of other learners and instructors creates the opportunity for both self- and other-affirmation. In addition, sharing becomes instructional for participants to the extent that it fosters reflection on and conversations about the content of what is being learned.

Portfolio Construction as Catalyst to Reflective Practice. As noted previously, artifacts and attestations that document learners' knowledge and understanding must be coupled with captions, explanatory statements, and reflective commentaries. These narrations define, provide the context, and analyze the individual and collective contents of the portfolio. Without these elaborations, a portfolio provides little context for purposeful and meaningful assessment, and it is at risk of being an unwieldy and esoteric scrapbook (Bird, 1990; Edgerton, Hutchings, and Quinlan, 1991; Wolf, 1991).

Especially important yet easily neglected in portfolio construction are *reflective commentaries*. Constructing reflective commentaries moves the learner beyond a description of the portfolio contents to an examination of the learning documented in the portfolio through a discussion of what the portfolio reveals about the learners' level of accomplishments. The form that these written reflections take can be left up to individual learners, or it can be structured by those involved in assessing the portfolio. Question prompts can assist learners in the task of assembling their material as well as provide a common focus for interactions with others. Examples of questions that might assist learners in constructing reflective statements include: What did I do? What does this mean? What have I learned? How might I do things differently? (Wellington, 1991). Written explanations and reflections by learners allow others to examine the thinking and decisions behind the accomplishments documented in the portfolio and enable those who review the portfolio to interpret its contents in meaningful ways.

Functions of Portfolio Assessment

Although variety seems to characterize the portfolio approach (Hutchings, 1990), the experiential learning model that represents the centerpiece for this work (Jackson and MacIsaac, Chapter Two) delineates three broad sets of assessment functions that portfolios can serve: (1) portfolios for self-assessment or reflection on personal growth; (2) portfolios that facilitate progress assessment within an educational program for adults; and (3) portfolios that enhance self-presentation to external sources (for example, portfolios for professional advancement on a job). Portfolios may serve a single function, thereby providing useful parameters for the selection of materials. However, it is also possible for portfolios to address several functions concurrently. The following sections, based in part on MacIsaac and Jackson (1992), detail these three key functions of the portfolio.

Portfolios for Self-Assessment. The process of developing a portfolio is as significant as the final product, in that through its construction learners have the opportunity to reflect on their learning as well as their professional and personal development. Because the portfolio provides a representation of personal growth, it can offer a foundation for goal setting and introspection. As a vehicle for self-assessment, a portfolio provides learners with opportunities to examine past work to determine how they have changed or grown as a consequence of a set of learning experiences.

As a structured and selective collection of materials that reflect a learner's accomplishments over time, portfolios also hold the potential for revealing patterns of personal knowledge construction and transformative learning over time. As learners review their portfolios, they gain insight into themselves as learners and see how different kinds of experiences have contributed to their learning process. Furthermore, as learners examine the final products represented in the portfolio in relation to current life challenges and work in progress, they can gain insights into personal areas of strength and areas in need of additional work.

In sum, portfolio construction can serve as a vehicle for self-assessment and self-reflection. It permits learners to constructively examine and critique the products as well as the processes of their own learning, and to revisit work accomplished in order to gain insights into their ongoing development and personal change. Portfolios can serve as powerful instructional as well as assessment tools as learners assume responsibility for assembling the evidence of change, engaging in self-assessment, and making decisions about the quality of their work. In so doing, learners come to realize in a very fundamental sense that they are ultimately responsible for their own learning (Tierney, Carter, and Desai, 1991).

Portfolios for Progress Assessment in Adult Learning Programs. When used to assess learners' progress within a program, a portfolio must include specific samples of material that reflect the attainment of the program's learning outcomes. In that portfolios can assume a variety of forms (Hutchings, 1990), it is useful to consider what progress assessment portfolios may have in common. We would suggest the following as a general guideline: a diverse range of works that represent various key activities in the program; work assigned by the instructors and work selected by the learner; an introduction in which the learner explains why individual pieces were chosen; a summary statement describing what was learned from the program and the portfolio assembly process (Johnson, 1991).

When applied to progress assessment, portfolios can be used in both a formative and summative manner. As a formative approach to assessment, the portfolio might include both learner- and instructor-selected items that represent learning in relation to program milestones, learner strengths and areas for improvement, and future learning directions. As a tool for formative assessment, the portfolio is a telling document, for it not only identifies certain ending points but also serves to illustrate how those end points were arrived at by the learner.

At the conclusion of a learning experience, portfolios can serve as a summative assessment to determine the extent to which learners have met specific goals and requirements. Such portfolios may contain not only learner-generated materials but also other documents required by the program or institution. Summative portfolios may also be used to assist learners in determining areas of strengths and weaknesses with respect to employment potential as well as continued training and further educational opportunities. Portfolios used within a context of program assessment are also a useful indicator of program effectiveness. That is, portfolios provide evidence that can be used in substantiating the degree to which an adult learning program is achieving its intended purpose.

Portfolios That Enhance Self-Presentation. Portfolios are also a way for learners to present themselves to others. Portfolios used in this way are often associated with seeking employment or additional educational and training opportunities. In such instances, learners select that material which best represents their competencies (for example, knowledge, skills, abilities, values, beliefs) in a given area or discipline. That is, a learner's portfolio would be specifically tailored to include those artifacts and attestations considered to be most germane and therefore the most revealing of one's qualities with regard to a particular set of external criteria. For example, a graphic artist might assemble a portfolio that includes actual samples of work representing skill in the use of various mediums and materials; photographs and videotapes of commissioned projects; a chronological vita documenting exhibits; certificates or degrees indicating training and professional preparation; and letters of recommendation and sponsorship from previous employers and professionals within the field. When used in this manner, the portfolio represents a tangible product that promotes the learner to prospective employers or indicates one's readiness for advanced training or education.

Learner Reflection in Portfolio Construction

The power of the portfolio process for assessing growth and change across time is clearly indicated in the foregoing discussion of portfolio functions. In this section, we would like to reemphasize that a portfolio is more than an activity record and offer additional examples to illustrate this.

A portfolio may be best conceived as an ongoing formative plan in which the learner sets goals, documents evidence of goal attainment, analyzes and reflects on changing knowledge, identifies areas for improvement, and establishes additional directions for continued growth. Hence, a portfolio is a vehicle for engaging learners in active reflection at three different levels.

At the most elementary level, a portfolio selectively documents the events, activities, or products that have been accomplished by learners. At this level of construction, the reflective commentaries that accompany samples of work are primarily labels, definitions, discussions of chronology, and explanatory descriptions of accomplishments and experiences. In other words, at this level, reflection is *remembering* what has been accomplished, when, and how.

Moving beyond descriptive accounts requires learners to analyze, interrelate, and synthesize their various accomplishments in relation to their learning. At this next level, the presentation of evidence moves beyond "here's what I have done" to "here's what all this means" with respect to a given portfolio function. The commentary that accompanies work at this level provides an opportunity for learners to reflect on the meaning of certain changes in their behaviors, beliefs, and values; establish the value of these changes for themselves and for other audiences; and analyze and synthesize the implications of these changes for their present activities and practices within a variety of activity and interpersonal contexts. Commentaries of this nature provide an authentic and multi-textured view of the actual learning experiences, as well as insights into the learner's process of thinking through the experiences that have taken place.

At the third and final level of reflection, a learner not only substantiates claims to learning through reflections and rationales, but also assumes greater responsibility for charting a future course for continued growth and learning. As Levi (1990) notes, assessment of learning must not stop with a review of work. Learners must articulate their hopes for the coming months and years. The learner who is reflecting at this level is active in formulating, implementing, and monitoring necessary next steps for professional and personal development. Thus, at this level, portfolios serve as springboards to future learning, enabling learners to revisit their accomplishments for purposes of making meaningful connections between completed works and proposed personal futures.

As part of a larger reflective process, it can be seen that portfolios can go beyond providing evidence of specific changes and their implications, becoming instead indices of a learner's personal and professional growth across the life span. In this sense, portfolios have the potential to extend beyond the boundaries of specific educational programs. This potential challenges educators of adults to consider how to assess learners within the broader context of their individual lives rather than narrowly in relation to the specific content of a class or program.

Conclusion

Portfolio assessment has been characterized as a form of assessment that is authentic, continuous, multidimensional, and interactive. Portfolios chronicle a learner's growth and understanding, and they provide opportunities for collaboration and reflection (Wiggins, 1989; Valencia, 1990). Portfolios portray a multi-textured view of learners, and they make visible both the processes and products involved in learning. As a process, portfolios are as useful as a means for learners to think through the connectedness of their ideas as they are for revealing how participants construct more complex ideas (Forrest, 1990).

The functions to be served by the portfolio determine to a large extent the types of information that are selected from the folio for inclusion within the portfolio. In this chapter we have outlined the following portfolio assessment functions: portfolios for self-assessment; portfolios that facilitate progress assessment within an adult learning program; and portfolios that enhance self-presentation to outside sources.

Regardless of purpose, the material within a portfolio should be more than a record of learning experiences and products. When accompanied by rich explanations and reflective commentary, a portfolio can document accomplishments and their chronology, the meaning and implications of specific accomplishments for the learner and for others, and a course of action for the future. As is evident from our discussion, the process of constructing portfolios can help develop in learners "the awareness and capacities for effective self monitoring and active reflection" (Smith, 1991, p. 12) and offer learners opportunities to assume greater responsibility for the content and assessment of their own learning from a life span perspective.

References

Arter, J. A., and Spandel, V. "NCME Instructional Module: Using Portfolios of Student Work in Instruction and Assessment." *Educational Measurement,* 1992, *11* (1), 36–44.

Barnett, B. G. "Using Alternate Assessment Measures in Educational Leadership Programs: Educational Platforms and Portfolios." *Journal of Personnel in Education,* 1992, *6,* 141–151.

Bird, T. "The School Teachers' Portfolio: An Essay on Possibilities." In J. Milman and L. Darling-Hammond (eds.), *The New Handbook of Teacher Evaluation: Assessing Elementary and Secondary School Teachers.* Newbury Park, Calif.: Sage, 1990.

Edgerton, R., Hutchings, P., and Quinlan, K. *The Teaching Portfolio: Capturing the Scholarship of Teaching.* Washington, D.C.: American Association for Higher Education, 1991.

Elbow, P., and Belanoff, P. "Portfolios as a Substitute for Proficiency Examinations." *College Composition and Communication,* 1986, *37* (3), 36–39.

ERIC Trends and Issues Alerts. *Portfolio Assessment in Adult, Career, and Vocational Education.* Columbus, Ohio: ERIC Clearinghouse on Adult, Career, and Vocational Education, 1993.

Forrest, A. *Time Will Tell.* Washington, D.C.: American Association for Higher Education, 1990.

Geiger, J., and Shugarman, S. "Portfolios and Case Studies to Evaluate Teacher Education Students and Programs." *Action in Teacher Education,* 1988, *10* (3), 31–34.

Graves, D. H., and Sunstein, B. S. *Portfolio Portraits.* Portsmouth, N.H.: Heinemann, 1992.

Hanson, J. "Literacy Portfolios: Helping Students Know Themselves." *Educational Leadership,* 1992, *49* (8), 66–68.

Hutchings, P. "Learning Over Time: Portfolio Assessment." *AAHE Bulletin,* 1990, *42* (8), 6–8.

Johnson, M. "Wedding Process to Product and Assessment to Learning." *Portfolio News,* 1991, *2* (3), 2.

Knight, P. "How I Use Portfolios in Mathematics." *Educational Leadership,* 1992, *49* (8), 71–72.

Levi, R. "Assessment and Educational Vision: Engaging Learners and Parents." *Language Arts,* 1990, *67* (3), 269–273.

MacIsaac, D., and Jackson, L. "Portfolio Assessment Processes and Outcomes." *Portfolio News,* 1992, *4* (1), 1–13.

Matthews, J. K. "From Computer Management to Portfolio Assessment." *The Reading Teacher,* 1990, *43* (4), 420–421.

O'Neil, J. "Portfolio Assessment Bears the Burden of Popularity." *ASCD Update,* 1993, *35* (8), 3–8.

Seldin, P. *The Teaching Portfolio: A Practical Guide to Improved Performance and Promotion/Tenure Decisions.* Bolton, Maine: Anker, 1991.

Shulman, L. "A Union of Insufficiencies: Strategies for Teacher Assessment in a Period of Educational Reform." *Educational Leadership,* 1988, *46* (3), 36–41.

Smith, R. M. "How People Become Effective Learners." *Adult Learning,* 1991, *2* (6) ,11–13.

Tierney, R., Carter, M. A., and Desai, E. *Portfolio Assessment in Reading-Writing Classrooms.* Norwood, Maine: Christopher-Gordon, 1991.

Valencia, S. "A Portfolio Approach to Classroom Reading Assessment: The Whys, Whats, and Hows." *The Reading Teacher,* 1990, *43* (4), 333–340.

Wellington, B. "The Promise of Reflective Practice." *Educational Leadership,* 1991, *48* (6), 4–5.

Wiggins, G. "A True Test: Toward More Authentic and Equitable Assessment." *Phi Delta Kappan,* 1989, *70* (9), 703–713.

Wolf, D. P. "Portfolio Assessment: Sampling Student Work." *Educational Leadership,* 1989, *46* (7), 35–39.

Wolf, K. P. "The School Teacher's Portfolio: Issues in Design, Implementation, and Evaluation." *Phi Delta Kappan,* 1991, *73* (2), 129–136.

DOUG MACISAAC is assistant professor in the Teacher Education Division at the University of Northern Colorado.

LEWIS JACKSON is associate professor in the Division of Special Education at the University of Northern Colorado.

Examples of applications of the experiential learning model, which is the centerpiece of this volume, in higher education and in the workplace are described.

Applying the Model to a Variety of Adult Learning Situations

Diane S. Bassett, Lewis Jackson

In their chapter on methods and techniques for engaging adult learners, Lee and Caffarella have shown that instructional activities adhering to experiential learning principles should provide a connection between the adults' prior experiences and the acquisition of new information. Adult learners bring a wealth of experiential knowledge to any learning situation, and it is the synthesis between this knowledge and new information and skills that defines the competence of participants who have completed a learning activity or program. Moreover, Barnett and Lee, followed by MacIsaac and Jackson, have shown that assessment must be an integral part of this learning process, providing a basis for participants and instructors alike to confirm and reflect on the learning and growth that has and is occurring.

Traditional educational programs for adults have often focused their instruction and assessment activities on information acquisition and problem solving, both of which reflect the application of analytical intelligence to the learning situation (Guskin, 1991). However, according to Sternberg (1988), individuals possess two additional types of intelligence: creative intelligence, which utilizes insight and the ability to synthesize a variety of conceptual tasks into a new framework; and adaptive intelligence, which emphasizes the learner's need for flexibility to deal with a changing environment. The learning and assessment activities that are prescribed by the model offered in this volume enhance knowledge acquisition by encouraging utilization of all three forms of intelligence. Learning is viewed as an adaptive process in which prior knowledge is *transformed* by means of a set of contextually valid learning experiences requiring creative and insightful examination of real world problems and applications. Moreover, the perspective on assessment that is incorporated in the model promotes a reflective process that ensures continued growth long after specific learning opportunities have been completed.

As more adults seek to improve their educational status through training programs, postsecondary degree programs, staff development, continuing education, or the pursuit of individual interests, we can expect to see a wider endorsement of the experiential learning concepts and principles that are represented in the model. This is especially so given that experiential concepts and techniques are already at least somewhat integrated into many facets of the adult learning experience. For example, colleges of business and industrial settings use large-scale simulations (LSS) to enhance communication and problem-solving skills (Albert, 1993). Many liberal arts colleges and universities, such as Antioch College, Prescott College, and Evergreen College, utilize experiential learning as the foundation of their programs. Professional development also incorporates experiential techniques through the use of technology, internships, simulations, and cooperative service to the community.

At the same time, what struck us in our review of the experiential and adult education literatures is that most discussions of exemplary programs describe applications of only certain facets of our model. In other words, there is a dearth of documentation on programs that reflect the kinds of consumer market analysis, conceptual planning, experiential teaching applications, and authentic assessment activities that, *when performed collectively,* represent the fullest expression of the promise of experiential learning. As proposed by Jackson and MacIsaac in Chapter Two, it is in the integration and synthesis of (1) knowledge about adult learners and the context of their lives; (2) conceptual foundations of experiential learning; (3) methods and techniques of experiential learning; and (4) authentic assessment practices that the potential of experiential learning is truly realized. We believe that our experiential learning model, which is reviewed in Figure 7.1, promotes just such an integration and synthesis of these concepts.

In this chapter, we illustrate ways in which the experiential learning and authentic assessment concepts that are represented in the model can be applied in a variety of adult learning contexts. We describe promising applications in higher education (teacher education and educational technology) and in the world of work (adventure programs, adult literacy, and diversity training). Our discussion identifies programs that exemplify selected facets of the model, and it illustrates at a hypothetical level how all of the components of the model can be employed collectively and in relation to each other. We begin with higher education.

Applications in Higher Education

As our understanding of adult growth and learning increases, more thought and energy is being directed into redesigning courses and programs that incorporate experiential techniques. Applications of experiential learning concepts in higher education can range from the modification of in-class experiences to

Figure 7.1. Proposed Experiential Learning Model

Characteristics and Needs of Adult Learners
Role of experience and prior knowledge
Differences in the processes of learning
Active involvement in the learning process
Affiliation needs of the learner
Context of adult lives

Conceptual Foundations of Experiential Learning
Definitions of knowledge
Elements of cognition
Constructivist teaching
Reflective practice
Context of learning

Methods and Techniques for Engaging Learners in
  Experiential Learning Activities
Design of in-class experiences
Design of field-based experiences
Coordination and integration of in-class and
  field-based experiences

Assessment Processes and Outcomes: Building a Folio
Artifacts
Reproductions
Attestations

Assessment Processes and Outcomes: Portfolio Construction
Self-assessment and self-reflection
Assessing learner progress in a program
Self-presentation to external sources

restructuring entire degree programs. For example, over twenty years ago, the 'K' Plan at Kalamazoo College was instituted for all liberal arts students. Students complete their degree requirements by drawing on a combination of career internship, study in a foreign country, a senior project that is individualized, and other cocurricular activities.

During any given year, students in this program spend 75 percent of their credit hours on campus and 25 percent off campus. The results have yielded graduates with lower unemployment rates and higher professional expectations; Kalamazoo has been ranked 14th of the top 100 undergraduate colleges in the production of students who subsequently acquire their Ph.D.s (Caccese, 1984).

Another program, Sea Semester, is sponsored by the Sea Education Association (a nonprofit organization) which receives partial funding through the National Science Foundation. Students spend a semester at sea studying oceanography, nautical science, and maritime history. Of the 2,000 university undergraduate students who have completed the semester, half go on to graduate school in marine science (Collison, 1989).

Programs such as the foregoing rely on constructivist teaching, reflective practice, and the use of valid contexts for learning as stalwarts of their instructional practices. However, nowhere are these concepts more evident than in cooperative education, in which students are required to try different work experiences, including community service, as part of their educational programs. Antioch College, for example, mandates that all students have six work experiences in different settings, including work experiences in settings that are unrelated to their major areas of interest. The University of Kentucky has institutionalized an Office of Experiential Education whose responsibilities include placing students for a maximum of 30 credit hours in off-campus internships in such areas as education, state government, medicine, and social work (Kendall and Associates, 1990). These innovations have capitalized on the premise that educational experiences must combine in-class activities with the kinds of concrete, authentic learning opportunities that only field-based experiences can offer.

The foregoing are just a few of the longstanding efforts that are occurring in higher education in which experiential learning and authentic assessment concepts and principles are being broadly applied. In the following subsections, we examine in detail two arenas of application: teacher education and educational technology. Our discussion reviews ongoing applications that are consistent with facets of our experiential learning model, and it shows how applications in higher education might be expanded to more fully express the components of the model.

Teacher Education. The possibilities for the use of experiential learning principles in teacher education are limitless. For example, at the University of Northern Colorado, there is a program designed to support and assist beginning and reentry teachers through a university-school partnership referred to as the Teacher Induction Partnerships program (MacIsaac, 1992). The program is a graduate level program in which teachers assume full instructional responsibilities in a classroom while receiving support and guidance from a university faculty member and a school-based mentor teacher.

As an integral part of their yearlong induction experience, the participants are involved in an ongoing professional development process. This process includes the construction of a professional development plan; attendance and participation in a yearlong series of university sponsored, school-based seminars; and the compilation of a teaching portfolio, which represents their knowledge and progress in teaching across the induction year. It has been observed that teachers participating in the portfolio development process tend to create their individual portfolios in one of the three formats identified in the model (Figure 7.1): self-reflection, self-presentation, or documentation of program progress. The choice of format appears to depend on the individual learner's professional and personal goals and expectations at the time the portfolio is assembled (Jackson and MacIsaac, 1991).

Figure 7.2 shows how the model components can be configured to represent issues in teacher education. One way the model can be used is to explore how items in one model component can affect other components. For example, as exemplified in "Characteristics and Needs of Adult Learners," because adult learners vary in their prior teaching experience, a blending of resources can occur by allowing experienced teachers to be mentors for beginning teachers ("Methods and Techniques for Engaging Learners in Experiential Learning Activities"). This information can again be put to use by individualizing the outcome expectations associated with the video assessment process described in "Assessment Processes and Outcomes: Building a Folio" to differentially challenge beginning and advanced teachers.

Educational Technology Applications. Educational technology, defined here as the use of computer-, video-, and audio-based technologies and telecommunication to enhance or make accessible learning opportunities, requires experiential learning practices if its application is to be meaningful and effective. When adults are viewed as self-directed learners with differing learning strengths and needs and whose prior knowledge and ongoing experiences can enhance new learning for the individual and other participants, educational technology becomes a powerful tool.

Figure 7.2. Applying the Experiential Learning Model: Teacher Preparation

Characteristics and Needs of Adult Learners
Differences in prior teaching experience
Differences in social supports in relation to child care responsibilities
Differences in career affiliation needs: "my own classroom" versus "collaborating with
    other teachers"

Conceptual Foundations of Experiential Learning
Different classroom decisions require different types of knowledge: quick decision
    knowledge ("knowing in action") versus constructed decision knowledge ("reflection-
    in-action")
Reflective practice as a fundamental teaching paradigm

Methods and Techniques for Engaging Learners in Experiential Learning Activities
Pairing experienced teachers returning to school with beginning teachers who have
    minimal experience in a mentor relationship
Listening groups focusing on learner presentations about how they assess student
    learning

Assessment Processes and Outcomes: Building a Folio
Videos of instructional interactions with students, completed at various points in the
    program
Documented peer reviews of classroom data collection activities

Assessment Processes and Outcomes: Portfolio Construction
Self-presentation portfolios that promote a teacher as team player, skilled technician in
    instructionally differentiated programming, and student advocate
Self-reflection portfolios that enhance a teacher's ability to assess current strengths and
    future professional development needs

The use of educational technology in combination with experiential learning is in evidence across numerous programs in higher education. Business classes, for example, combine simulations and the setting up of actual businesses to lend relevance to course content (Nappi, 1986); computer applications are an integral part of this process. In law schools, moot court (simulated courtroom activities) has long been a standard part of instruction, but law courses are also providing clinics and interactive immersion in real cases as part of their requirements (Burman, 1992; Robinson, 1992). This process can include using videos to take depositions and using databases, such as LEXUS, to determine prior case law.

Distance learning is an application where, through technology, learning takes place in the communities of the learners. Instruction can be especially relevant as students can integrate local knowledge with information from afar. One project, the Annenberg/CPB Project, has funded seven postsecondary institutions to develop academic programs using technologies for distance delivery. The University of Maine at Augusta, for instance, is a community college system which serves more than 5,000 students across the state using computer software, videodiscs, and satellite transmission. Fourteen associate degree programs are offered, all of which transfer to four-year institutions within the state (Smith-Davis, 1992). As an example of the use of experiential learning as part of distance learning, a biology professor mails out fetal pigs for dissection. The pigs are dissected at the site while viewing a demonstration delivered via satellite communication, and then are returned to the instructor with the appropriate organs labeled.

Figure 7.3 illustrates how the model can be configured to issues associated with educational technology so that important needs and relationships are revealed. For example, learners in rural communities located far from higher education centers benefit from satellite-transmitted programs because such programs assure access to educational resources (see in combination "Characteristics and Needs of Adult Learners" and "Methods and Techniques for Engaging Learners in Experiential Learning Activities"). Moreover, the model's configuration of the issues also indicates that meaningful and relevant learning can be enhanced in distance education because interactive, satellite-transmitted classes provide a means for learners in isolated communities who have common work and social contexts to share with each other reflections and solutions to problems that they are experiencing (see "Conceptual Foundations of Experiential Learning").

Applications in the Workplace

American businesses spend around $60 billion annually on both formal and informal training (Gass, Goldman, and Priest, 1992). In meeting the training needs of employees, businesses have entered into a wide array of cooperative agreements with schools, libraries, and other agencies that can provide experientially based educational programs (Wiswell, 1990). For example, the Coun-

Figure 7.3. Applying the Experiential Learning Model: Educational Technology

Characteristics and Needs of Adult Learners
Differences in contexts of adult lives: "I need to stay in my community" versus "I can travel to take classes"
Differences in knowledge and experience with educational technology
Differences in social needs during learning: learning by oneself or need for affiliation with others

Conceptual Foundations of Experiential Learning
Learners sharing similar work and community contexts can enhance one another's learning.
Autonomous self-directed learning demands use of reflective practices.

Methods and Techniques for Engaging Learners in Experiential Learning Activities
Debates and discussions across learning sites via satellite transmission
Field experiences that reflect local community issues, shared by means of conference calls with learners at other sites
Computer-mediated conferencing and bulletin boards for sharing information
Applied simulations, as in market analysis and medical procedures

Assessment Processes and Outcomes: Building a Folio
Videos of learners engaging in assigned task
Completed workshop in utilizing various forms of technology, such as videodiscs and computers, documented by a certificate of completion

Assessment Processes and Outcomes: Portfolio Construction
Self-presentation portfolios that demonstrate the way the learner has acquired content through the use of computers and other media

cil for Adult and Experiential Learning (CAEL) provides comprehensive employee education and training through its joint venture model. Under this model, CAEL acts as a bridge between employer, employees, and educational providers to provide services (CAEL, 1992). It draws these groups together into a partnership to develop an integrated educational and training plan specific to the training and personnel needs of the organization. Training is then delivered through a variety of means: workshops, simulations, use of technology, and so forth. Organizations utilizing such personalized training have enjoyed increases in productivity and decreases in employee turnover. CAEL cites an example of one fast food chain where high turnover cost the company $62,000 in yearly training and hiring costs at one site. After an investment of $10,000 for instructional training fees, turnover was dramatically reduced to 58 percent (versus 240 percent for other similar sites) (CAEL, 1992).

In this section we examine in detail three arenas for model application in the world of the workplace: adventure programs, adult literacy programs, and diversity training. As in the section on higher education, our discussion shows how certain ongoing applications of experiential learning are consistent with facets of the experiential learning model as well as how future applications might be expanded to take into account the full implications of the model.

Adventure Programs. As discussed by Lewis and Williams (Chapter One), a popular training avenue is the use of outdoor education to enhance team building, leadership development, and organizational change. Through challenging outdoor activities, participants are required to use problem solving, leadership, cooperation, and communication skills with the assumption that these skills will generalize to their working environments. The Breckenridge Outdoor Education Center in Colorado is well known for its application of experiential learning to the business sector. Companies send their employees to the center to engage in ropes courses, orienteering, and other problem-solving activities. These exercises exemplify teaming strengths and needs in an immediate way, which can then be addressed in the learning process ("Outdoor Education," 1993).

Adventure training capitalizes on prior knowledge and experience and individual ways of knowing to create an intense learning process that is rich in growth opportunities. An outdoor problem-solving exercise, for example, may be directly tied to the team building necessary for productivity in the workplace by assigning individuals together based on their expected workplace relationships.

Figure 7.4 illustrates how experiential learning concepts and activities that are routinely used in adventure programming (Nadler and Luckner, 1992) can be integrated into the general framework of our model to reveal useful relationships between the components. For example, instructors may implement spontaneous "risk" experiences designed to promote group cohesiveness ("Methods and Techniques for Engaging Learners in Experiential Learning Activities"). These experiences would be based on their knowledge of the social needs of individual participants (see "Characteristics and Needs of Adult Learners") in combination with their understanding of how relationships form in cooperative work groups (see "Conceptual Foundations of Experiential Learning").

Adult Literacy Programs. Businesses are recognizing the need for enhanced literacy skills in their workers. Many U.S. corporations have formed partnerships with postsecondary institutions and literacy projects to aid workers in upgrading their literacy skills. Companies are recognizing that poor literacy skills increase production costs. In 1988, for example, JLG Industries reported spending over one million dollars to correct worker literacy mistakes (Cornell, 1988). Moreover, Mikulecky (1984) reports that the Department of Labor's projections for future vocations cite the disappearance of many occupations that do not require literacy.

It is within this context that experiential learning can aid in a renaissance of literacy training. One such project employing experiential learning principles is the Westonka Project. Located in a 2,000 square mile area west of Minneapolis, the project is sponsored by a consortium of fourteen school districts and the National Issues Forum (NIF) Literacy Project. Twenty-six community sites (including two county jails) offer basic literacy instruction, including Eng-

**Figure 7.4. Applying the Experiential Learning Model:
Adventure Programming**

Characteristics and Needs of Adult Learners
Differences in need to feel a part of a team or group
Differences in risk tolerance: cautious individuals versus risk takers

Conceptual Foundations of Experiential Learning
Typical patterns in the formation of interpersonal relationships within cooperative work
    groups
Levels of processing in learning: awareness, assuming responsibility, active experimenta-
    tion, and generalization/transfer
Metaphors and stories as bases for learning and transfer of learning
Disequilibrium/knowledge breakthroughs in constructive processing

Methods and Techniques for Engaging Learners in Experiential Learning Activities
Instructor-initiated "risk" experiences, planned spontaneously in response to emerging
    needs of the participants, that can facilitate the experience of significant personal
    growth ("planned chance events")
Debriefing sessions focusing on real-world applications of learning

Assessment Processes and Outcomes: Building a Folio
Journal writing, in which participants are directed to relate adventure programming expe-
    riences to significant challenges in the workplace (for example, managing disagree-
    ments in survival partnerships compared to managing disagreements in corporate-level
    teaming)
A letter attesting to a colleague's change in corporate teaming skills

Assessment Processes and Outcomes: Portfolio Construction
Integrating photographs, poetry, journal entries, and other items into a more broadly
    based professional portfolio so that specific, job-relevant skills of the program partici-
    pant are made apparent

lish as a second language. Using resources provided by the NIF, the participants read and discuss policy issues including national security, welfare, crime,
and the farm crisis (Hurley, 1991). Because these issues are learner-relevant
and are presented through both reading and open discussion, reflective and
active participation in learning is enhanced.

The Kentucky Educational Television (KET) operates a wide range of
instructional television programming to improve citizen literacy skills. The
KET/GED Series is an instructional program providing 43 half-hour video
lessons for adults across the U.S. preparing for the Graduate Equivalency
Diploma (GED). The series utilizes workbooks to parallel the videos as well as
computer-aided instruction to reinforce what is being learned. The use of technology provides a conduit for students to learn in their homes or in their work-
places. KET/GED also offers a program entitled "Learn to Read" for adults who
are nonreaders. Using a phonetic approach to emphasize sound-symbol relationships, the series offers 30 half-hour video lessons supplemented with 87
audio lessons. The use of these video and audio materials, in conjunction with

individualized workbooks, gives students control over the pace of their learning (Smith-Davis, 1992).

Figure 7.5 illustrates how the experiential learning model can be broadly applied to a variety of issues related to adult literacy. As shown in Figure 7.5, the model provides a succinct framework for conceptualizing the full gamut of literacy issues, from the unique needs of specific learners through the processes of authentic assessment and the promotion of learners in the workplace. For example, individual differences in literacy needs (see "Characteristics and Needs of Adult Learners") can translate into different types of personal portfolios during assessment processes (see "Assessment Processes and Outcomes: Portfolio Construction").

Diversity Training. Jackson and MacIsaac (Chapter Two) point out in their discussion of the needs of adult learners that cultural, gender, ethnic, and life-style diversity are increasing in today's work force and in society at large. Indeed, as noted by Greene (1993), it is becoming "increasingly indefensible to structure knowledge monologically"; we must recognize "the existence of

**Figure 7.5. Applying the Experiential Learning Model:
Adult Literacy Programs**

Characteristics and Needs of Adult Learners
Differences in literacy needs (for example, "survival literacy skills" versus "reading complex novels for pleasure"); differences in reading interests ("sports" versus "cookbooks")
Differences in personal histories with respect to prior schooling
Differences in subcultural perceptions of "remedial" instruction

Conceptual Foundations of Experiential Learning
Different kinds of materials provide very different contexts for learning, and these can profoundly affect learner responsiveness (for example, age-inappropriate materials can serve as a disincentive).
Different cultural backgrounds result in different understandings of the same narrative passages.

Methods and Techniques for Engaging Learners in Experiential Learning Activities
Analysis of personal literacy practices in workplace and leisure settings, followed by development of a professional development plan
Individualized, adult computer games requiring some reading to play

Assessment Processes and Outcomes: Building a Folio
Personal letters that illustrate changing writing skills
Passages from reflective journaling on growing-up experiences and their impact on current thinking and behavior

Assessment Processes and Outcomes: Portfolio Construction
Program assessment portfolios configured to the specific occupational needs of the learner (for example, completed job applications for a welder who is completing an English as second language course)
Self-assessment portfolio that includes extensive autobiographical narrative and reflective commentary

many voices, some contesting, some cohering, all demanding and deserving attention" (p. 212).

The acceptance of differences, indeed the celebration of diversity, is emerging as a key issue in the education of adult learners (Ross-Gordon, 1991). However, its relevance extends well beyond adult education practices. It is a critical issue for any and all citizens who must now be able to collaborate with people who do not, and need not, possess the same world views as themselves. As noted by Fowler (1986), "rapid communication, the tele-media, increased mobility, and other late-twentieth century phenomena are creating a global economy" (p. 72). This global economy invariably affects the social ecologies of persons who must now work together but who lack the linguistic, attitudinal, and cultural commonalities that engender ease of association.

Within this changing social and economic climate, businesses will increasingly need diversity and equity training (that is, cultural and gender bias awareness) to enhance the interpersonal and intercultural communicative effectiveness and, ultimately, the productivity of their work forces. This training can involve simulations, speakers, participation in community service, and problem-solving scenarios. However, if it is to promote meaningful change, it is imperative that the learning activities engage participants in a process in which new perspectives and information are learned in relation to each learner's own personal tasks and needs. As noted by Fowler (1986), simulation games may be especially useful in this regards. Games such as BAFÁ BAFÁ connect learners in nonthreatening ways with skills and perceptions that can increase both their sensitivity to and interpersonal effectiveness with other cultures and peoples.

Figure 7.6 illustrates how the experiential learning model can be used to represent key issues, techniques, and conceptual relationships in diversity training. As an example of how this representation can promote decision making, consider the interrelationship between "differences in amount of contact with dissimilar cultural groups" (see "Characteristics and Needs of Adult Learners") and the theoretical implications of heterogeneous groups (see "Conceptual Foundations of Experiential Learning") as these two issues relate to "Methods and Techniques for Engaging Learners in Experiential Learning Activities." Heterogeneous group compositions may be quite important with learners who have had minimal contact with cultures other than their own; it may be less of an issue with learners who have a broad experiential base with other cultures, but need specific information to deal with a specific culture or ethnic group.

Conclusion

We have illustrated in this chapter some ways in which the experiential learning model that is described in this volume can be applied in a variety of adult learning contexts. We have described some promising applications in higher education, specifically in teacher education and educational technology, and in the workplace, specifically in adventure programs, adult literacy programs,

Figure 7.6. Applying the Experiential Learning Model: Diversity Training

Characteristics and Needs of Adult Learners
Differences in amount of contact with dissimilar cultural groups
Differences in experienced social and economic pressures that sustain ethnic prejudice and/or cultural ethnocentrism
Differences in motivation to change social and attitudinal views

Conceptual Foundations of Experiential Learning
The context of instruction: heterogeneous versus homogeneous group composition in different learning activities

Methods and Techniques for Engaging Learners in Experiential Learning Activities
Members of group representing minority cultures share their experiences with a listening group.
Symposiums that explore factors that contribute to ethnic prejudice
Role assumption exercises, in which participants place themselves in situations where they encounter some of the prejudices that a particular group is accustomed to experiencing (for example, learners spend time with groups in which they are the minority members)

Assessment Processes and Outcomes: Building a Folio
Products of modeling activities; for example, conceptual maps that interrelate a participant's personal perceptions, attitudes, and feelings about other cultures, religions, or life-styles

Assessment Processes and Outcomes: Portfolio Construction
Self-assessment portfolios that reflect changes in attitudes or perceptions
Self-presentation portfolios that include evidence that a person is sensitive to and respects cultural diversity and human rights (for example, portfolio includes testimonials and service awards)

and diversity training. We have also shown at a hypothetical level how all of the components of the model can be used in conjunction with each other as a conceptual tool in the design and implementation of programs and learning activities for adult learners.

Reflecting on our hypothetical examples, we can describe a 4-step process for applying the model in the design of programs and learning activities. First, the content area (for example, diversity training) is identified and defined. Second, by means of market research, library research, field surveys, personal reflection, and/or group brainstorming, all the model components (such as "Conceptual Foundations of Experiential Learning") are "filled in" with information relevant to the program or learning activity. Third, interrelationships between the model components are identified using three reflective tools: (1) top-down analysis (moving sequentially from the higher components of the model down into the lower components); (2) bottom-up analysis (moving sequentially from the lower components of the model up to the higher components); and (3) eclectic analysis (comparing and contrasting any model component with any other component). Fourth and finally, the implications of the inter-component relationships are brought to bear on the program or learning activity that is being designed. That is, instructional content, experiential learning activities, and assessment techniques are selected or modified according to what the analysis revealed. In sum, by systematically examining interrelationships between the components of the experiential learning model, educators can enhance the authenticity and value of their learning activities and programs for adult learners.

References

Albert, F. "Large-Scale Simulation in Marketing Education." *Journal of Marketing Education,* 1993 (Summer), 307–335.

Burman, J. M. "Out-of-Class Assignments as a Method of Teaching and Evaluating Law Students." *Journal of Legal Education,* 1992, *42* (3), 447–457.

Caccese. A. "The Kalamazoo Plan: Institutionalizing Internships for Liberal Arts Students." *Innovative Higher Education,* 1984, *9* (2), 59–75.

Collison, M. "A Semester at Sea: Students Learn Nautical Science, Oceanography, and Which Line Lowers the Topsail." *Chronicle of Higher Education,* May 3, 1989, pp. A33–A34.

Cornell, T. "Characteristics of Effective Occupational Literacy Programs." *Journal of Reading,* 1988, *31* (7), 654–656.

Council for Adult and Experiential Learning. *Closing the Skills Gap: New Solutions.* Chicago: ERIC Reproduction Service, 1992. (ED 353 397)

Fowler, S. M. "Intercultural Simulation Games: Removing Cultural Blinders." In L. H. Lewis (ed.), *Experiential and Simulation Techniques for Teaching Adults.* New Directions for Continuing Education, no. 30. San Francisco: Jossey-Bass, 1986.

Gass, M., Goldman, K., and Priest, S. "Constructing Effective Adventure Training Programs." *Journal of Experiential Education,* 1992, *15* (1), 35–42.

Greene, M. "Diversity and Inclusion: Toward a Curriculum for Human Beings." *Teachers College Record,* 1993, *95* (2), 211–221.

Guskin, A. E. "On Changing Fundamental Conceptions of the Undergraduate Experience: Experiential Learning and Theories of Intelligence." *Journal of Cooperative Education,* 1991, *28* (2), 22–28.

Hurley, M. "Empowering Adult Learners." *Adult Learning,* 1991, *2* (4), 20–27.

Jackson, L. B., and MacIsaac, D. "Partner-Teacher Portfolio/Action Research Project Presentation." University of Northern Colorado Teacher Induction Partnerships Program Conference, Greeley, Colo., Apr. 1991.

Kendall, J. C., and Associates. *Combining Learning and Service.* Raleigh, N.C.: National Society for Internships and Experiential Learning, 1990.

MacIsaac, D. "The Teacher Induction Partnerships Program (TIP): A Collaborative Model for Teacher Induction Involving the University of Northern Colorado and Numerous Colorado School Districts." Paper presented at the annual meeting of the Association for Teacher Educators, Orlando, Fla., Feb. 1992.

Mikulecky, L. "Preparing Students for Workplace Literacy Demands." *Journal of Reading,* 1984, *28,* 253–257.

Nadler, R. S., and Luckner, J. L. *Processing the Adventure Experience: Theory and Practice.* Dubuque, Iowa: Kendall/Hunt, 1992.

Nappi, A. T. "Teaching Small Business Through Experiential Learning." *Journal of Education for Business,* 1986, *61* (5), 224–225.

"Outdoor Education: Breckenridge Center." *Ability,* 1993, *3* (4), 1215.

Robinson, T. A. "Simulated Legal Education: A Template." *Journal of Legal Education,* 1992, 42 (2), 296–298.

Ross-Gordon, J. M. "Needed: A Multicultural Perspective for Adult Education Research." *Adult Education Quarterly,* 1991, 42, 1–16.

Smith-Davis, J. "Distance Education: A Program Review." Unpublished manuscript, Outreach Alliance 2000 project, University of New Mexico, Albuquerque, 1992.

Sternberg, R. J. *The Triarchic Mind.* New York: Penguin Books, 1988.

Wiswell, A. K. "Business and Industry for Continuous Learning." In M. W. Galbraith (ed.), *Education Through Community Organizations.* New Directions for Adult and Continuing Education, no. 47. San Francisco: Jossey-Bass, 1990.

DIANE S. BASSETT is assistant professor in the Division of Special Education at the University of Northern Colorado.

LEWIS JACKSON is associate professor in the Division of Special Education at the University of Northern Colorado.

The experiential learning model is reviewed, and four implications for implementation and future research are discussed.

Implementation Issues and Future Research Directions

Lewis Jackson, Rosemary S. Caffarella

This volume of *New Directions for Adult and Continuing Education* has examined a new model for conceptualizing experiential learning theory in educational programs for adult learners. As described by Jackson and MacIsaac (Chapter Two), the model is a process model: It supports the design, implementation, and revision of learning activities and programs in which the conceptual underpinnings of experiential learning, the characteristics and needs of learners, and current methods and techniques for instruction and assessment are considered conjointly.

In Chapter One, Lewis and Williams reviewed the origins of experiential learning and discussed its present status. Next, the complete model was introduced by Jackson and MacIsaac (Chapter Two). Descriptions of the model's components were then provided in Chapters Three through Six: conceptual issues in experiential learning and the characteristics and needs of adult learners (Caffarella and Barnett); methods and techniques for engaging learners in experiential learning (Lee and Caffarella); assessment processes and outcomes in building a folio (Barnett and Lee); and assessment processes/outcomes in portfolio construction (MacIsaac and Jackson). Finally, Bassett and Jackson (Chapter Seven) discussed model applications in a variety of higher education and workplace settings.

Along with presenting technical information on how to use the model, these chapters touched on a number of emerging issues related to the advancement of experiential learning in the education of adult learners, including the importance of understanding and applying multiple theoretical perspectives to practice, concerns about the transfer of learning, implications of authentic assessment for traditional assessment practices, and cultural and ethnic issues in adult education. In this final chapter, we discuss in detail four issues, derived from discussions in earlier chapters, that are especially significant points of departure for the future study and practice of experiential learning in the education of adult learners: (1) experiential learning and human diversity, (2) experiential learning and social affiliation patterns, (3) experiential learning and transfer of learning, and (4) experiential learning and authentic assessment. We begin with experiential learning and human diversity.

Experiential Learning and Human Diversity

Perhaps one of the most notable themes in all of the chapters is that adult educators must configure learning activities and programs such that they respect and preserve the integrity of learners with different backgrounds and enhance the ways in which adult learners, in turn, respect and preserve the integrity of coworkers, customers, and others in their daily lives. This process, however, is made difficult by the sheer complexity of the interaction between cultural, ethnic, linguistic, gender, ability/disability, and life-style variables. Even the most determined adult educator will experience uncertainties when trying to apply current multicultural knowledge and perspectives to the tasks of instruction and assessment. It is not that becoming informed about diversity is not an important part of being an educator of adults; indeed, becoming aware of differences and how they affect learning is a vital step in any educational program that adheres to the principles of experiential learning. What cannot be overlooked, however, is that individual learners must be approached on their own terms, taking into account their unique needs, fears, and aspirations in activity and program design decisions. This point is illustrated in the instructional methods chapter by Lee and Caffarella and the assessment chapters by Barnett and Lee and by MacIsaac and Jackson, which demonstrate ways learning activities and assessment methods can be configured to meet the needs of individual learners. This idea of responding to learner diversity is also implicit in Lewis and Williams' discussion of the reflective learning cycle, which emphasizes how individual learners regulate their own knowledge acquisition process. Finally, this point is relevant to the Bassett and Jackson discussion of diversity training: Adult educators lay the foundations for instructing others in human differences in the ways they themselves honor the unique experiential backgrounds of their learners.

A concept that we believe offers insights into how educators of adults can approach learners more as individuals and less as members of a population is the social anthropological notion of *face*. Brown and Levinson (1978) describe face as "something that is emotionally invested, and that can be lost, maintained, or enhanced, and must be constantly attended to in interaction" (p. 66). By approaching adult learners as social beings who express in their interactions a fundamental need to show what is best and strong about themselves (positive face) and to protect themselves from experiences that impair self-image (negative face), educators of adults can express greater sensitivity to individual needs and characteristics in program and activity design decisions. This is because interpreting face requires actively listening to the implicit and explicit messages in the communications of learners, then reconfiguring learning activities and programs such that the voices in these messages are honored. In the language of Stephen Covey (1989), we become *emphatic listeners,* seeking first to understand and acknowledge the messages of others before making our own voices heard.

Experiential Learning and Social Affiliation Patterns

Caffarella and Barnett discuss in Chapter Three the importance of affiliation needs of adult learners in the design of learning activities and educational programs, and this is the second issue that is important to further explore. As was the case with human diversity, threads of this issue can be seen running through several of the chapters in this volume. For example, Lee and Caffarella point out that the value of storytelling as an instructional device can be enhanced when stories are told in a social context of mutual support and appreciation. For many who work with adult learners who are already practicing professionals, the process in which instructors and participants validate each others' experiences can sometimes be as important as new learning. Validation lends authenticity to the activities of participants, many of whom may be experiencing uncertainty because of lack of support in their professional settings.

As Caffarella and Barnett note, social affiliation patterns in the learning process have been receiving more attention in recent years. Perhaps this reflects a growing recognition that emotional and affective processes should not be treated as if they are independent of, or secondary to, the cognitive and intellectual processes of learners. For example, a reappraisal of Abraham Maslow's (1970) hierarchy of needs by persons involved in disability advocacy is revealing that educational programs often fail to recognize that the need for acceptance and group membership may be more basic than the need to experience achievement, which is often promoted as the essential ingredient in educational success. For many learners, concern for their learning difficulties may need to be reframed as a concern for whether they are experiencing adequate social support and peer acceptance (Kunc, 1992). Although this insight is emerging primarily in disability advocacy within public schools, the Caffarella and Barnett discussion makes it clear that it is relevant to programs for adults as well.

Experiential Learning and Transfer of Learning

Transfer of learning, defined by Caffarella (in press) as the effective application of what has been learned in a program to other life situations, is the third issue we view as especially significant. As noted by Jackson and MacIsaac in Chapter Two, this is one of the most important issues that needs to be considered when designing experiential learning activities and programs. The significance of this issue is also apparent in Lewis and Williams' discussion of concerns about the practical relevance and value of outdoor education; in Lee and Caffarella's discussion of ways to enhance experiential learning techniques to increase skill transfer; and in Bassett and Jackson's illustrations of instruction and assessment procedures that acknowledge the issue of *relevance of learning* for real-world settings. Collectively, these discussions indicate that designers and instructors of formal programs must examine closely the ways their instruction and assessment activities contribute to the professional and social skill demands confronting learners in real-world settings.

Two factors are relevant to the view that transfer of learning must become a more important concern in formal programs for adult learners. First, as discussed in the Lee and Caffarella discussion of the coordination of in-class and field-based experiences (Chapter Four), in-class activities are sometimes allotted too much emphasis in formal programs given what we know about transfer of learning. The field-based components of a program, such as internships and apprenticeships, should become as important or in some cases the primary focus in many formal programs, especially in human services and education.

Second, given the importance of social affiliation patterns, formal programs should consider as part of their charge the creation of social support networks for their participants. In the past, the fostering of participant relationships which endure after a formal program is over has been largely neglected or left mostly to chance. Yet, it is likely that activities such as the reciprocal sharing of experiences and information, the mutual provision of emotional support, and the development of professional and personal identity through continued contacts with peers are as necessary for skill transfer as being able to demonstrate critical competencies. In other words, evidence of a successful educational program can be the presence of an active network of relationships, and not just whether individual learners have acquired or are using certain skills and values.

Experiential Learning and Authentic Assessment

One of the most important messages of the Barnett and Lee and the MacIsaac and Jackson chapters is that authentic tools of assessment must become part of how adult learners and educators evaluate growth and change. This provides the fourth and final issue for this discussion.

Modern society is dependent on tests and assessment procedures that lack authenticity. These instruments tend to emphasize uniformity instead of individual uniqueness in performance competency and independent skill attainment instead of acculturation and interdependency as the measured outcomes of instruction. Put in another way, typical assessment procedures used in assessing readiness for a given role or occupation (for example, an objective test following a budgeting workshop) are not designed to assess the adaptation of individuals with unique characteristics and capabilities to particular environments, nor do they consider the accommodation of particular environments to the unique qualities of individuals.

Folio/portfolio assessment establishes a new direction for assessment in which both learner uniqueness and the "particularness" of relevant environments are acknowledged in the measurement process. Letters that attest to an individual's abilities, videos of an individual performing certain professional functions, and resume-style chronologies of an individual's professional and related experiences have in common the following: They provide measures of success that are sensitive to individual uniqueness and are grounded in the social and work settings that represent the contexts of the assessment process.

Typical objections to the foregoing kinds of assessment are that these performance indicators do not allow comparison of the individual's performance to uniform performance standards, and the measures are dependent on context for interpretation. However, these objections are grounded in two questionable assumptions: that objective performance standards have an enduring and valid relationship to human roles and activities, and that there is such a thing as context-free learning. The chapters in this volume suggest that a new paradigm may be emerging in our understanding of human learning, one which challenges fundamentally these views. The significant parameters of this paradigm are that (1) change is an ever-present feature of contemporary social and workplace settings, and change requires intermittent revision of performance expectations; and (2) inevitable differences in context require learners to reconfigure their conduct and skill performance in relation to the conditions of context. Folio and portfolio assessment procedures are well suited to this new paradigm, because they can reflect individual adaptations to change and to the conditions of specific contexts.

Final Reflections

Four issues for research and practice that are based on the experiential learning model presented in this volume have been discussed in this chapter. These issues are (1) understanding and honoring human diversity at the level of the individual learner; (2) the importance of social affiliation patterns for adult education programs; (3) the significant role that must be played by transfer of learning in teaching and assessment; and (4) the emerging importance of authentic assessment. Each issue is important in its own right for future research and practice in experiential learning.

However, there is also a point of convergence: Each of these issues promotes viewing learners as unique individuals who must use their acquired knowledge within specific social and material contexts in different ways. This idea, which we believe is inherent in the model itself, challenges more traditional views of learning, which tend to emphasize learner uniformities in the outcomes of instruction and de-emphasize the role of context in adult learning.

References

Brown, P., and Levinson, S. "Universals in Language Usage: Politeness Phenomena." In E. N. Goody (ed.), *Questions and Politeness: Strategies in Social Interaction.* Cambridge, England: Cambridge University Press, 1978.

Caffarella, R. S. *Planning Programs for Adult Learners: A Practical Guide for Educators, Trainers, and Staff Developers.* San Francisco: Jossey-Bass, in press.

Covey, S. R. *The 7 Habits of Highly Effective People.* New York: Simon & Schuster, 1989.

Kunc, N. "The Need to Belong: Rediscovering Maslow's Hierarchy of Needs." In R. A. Villa, J. S. Thousand, W. Stainback, and S. Stainback (eds.), *Restructuring for Caring and Effective Education: An Administrative Guide to Creating Heterogeneous Schools.* Baltimore: Brookes, 1992.

Maslow, A. *Motivation and Personality.* New York: HarperCollins, 1970.

LEWIS JACKSON is associate professor in the Division of Special Education at the University of Northern Colorado.

ROSEMARY S. CAFFARELLA is professor in the Division of Educational Leadership and Policy Studies at the University of Northern Colorado.

INDEX

ACE. *See* American Council on Education
Action learning technique, 10–12, 50–51
Adaptive intelligence, 73
Adult learners: affiliation patterns of, 32–33, 89, 90; characteristics and needs of, 20–22, 30–35, 75, 77, 79, 81, 82, 84, 89; control and responsibility, 32, 38, 44, 69–70; feelings of, 33–34, 38, 52, 88–89; five major characteristics of, 30–35; five types of, 21, 31; mindful, 39; responsibility for folios, 60–61; as unique individuals, 21–22, 25, 44, 70, 88–89, 91; women, 9, 18–19, 30, 33. *See also* Contexts of adult learning
Adult literacy programs, 80–82
Adventure training programs, 13–14, 80
Affiliation needs of learners, 32–33, 89, 90
Alternatives to formal assessment. *See* Portfolio construction
American Council on Education (ACE), 8
Analytical intelligence, 73
Antioch College, 76
Applications, model. *See* Experiential learning model applications
Apprenticeship, 37, 52
Apps, J. W., 32
Argyris, C., 11
Artifacts, assessment, 57–59. *See also* Folio, building a
Artist portfolios, 69
Assessment folios. *See* Folio, building a
Assessment portfolios. *See* Portfolios, learning
Assessment processes and outcomes, 18, 20, 75, 91; prior learning credit, 8; standardized tests, 18, 25, 56, 90–91; three changes from typical, 27. *See also* Portfolio construction
Attestations, other people's, 57–59, 91
Authentic assessment, 55–57, 90–91

Barba, M. P., 57
Barnett, B., 38–39, 63
Barton, J., 57, 60
Baskett, H.K.M., 31
Belanoff, P., 66
Belenky, M. F., 9, 30, 33
Bird, T., 57, 59, 66, 67

Blank, W. E., 31
Bolt, J. F., 10
Boud, D., 23, 35
Breckenridge Outdoor Education Center in Colorado, 80
Brookfield, S. D., 17, 30, 32, 33, 37, 39
Brown, P., 88
Buckmaster, A., 37
Building a folio. *See* Folio, building a
Bunsen, T., 22
Business training programs, 37, 46, 53, 65–66, 78–83

CAEL. *See* Council for the Advancement of Experiential Learning
Caffarella, R. S., 22, 30, 32, 33, 43, 49, 58, 89
Candy, P. C., 17, 22, 23, 37, 44
Carrolton, E. T., 57
Carter, M. A., 63, 68
Case, R., 56, 57
Case study analysis, 47, 49
Cavaliere, L. A., 31
Cervero, R. M., 35, 39
Change: adaptation to, 1, 18, 91; assessing transitional, 26. *See also* Portfolio construction
Characteristics and needs of adult learners: applications of, 75, 77, 79, 81, 82, 84; experiential learning model of, 20–22, 30–35, 75
Chi, M.T.H., 36
Chickering, A. W., 8, 9
Cizek, G. J., 18
Clark, M. C., 31
Classroom-based experiential learning, 8–10, 45–51
Claxton, C. S., 9
Clinchy, B. M., 9, 30, 33
Clinical supervision, 53
Clinics, practice problem, 53
Coaching, 52
Cognition, elements of, 23, 36–37
Collaboration, learning, 24, 33, 59
Collard, S., 33
College Level Education Program (CLEP), 8
Colleges, experiential learning in, 74, 76

ORDERING INFORMATION

NEW DIRECTIONS FOR ADULT AND CONTINUING EDUCATION is a series of paperback books that explores issues of common interest to instructors, administrators, counselors, and policy makers in a broad range of adult and continuing education settings—such as colleges and universities, extension programs, businesses, the military, prisons, libraries, and museums. Books in the series are published quarterly in Spring, Summer, Fall, and Winter and are available for purchase by subscription and individually.

SUBSCRIPTIONS for 1994 cost $47.00 for individuals (a savings of 25 percent over single-copy prices) and $62.00 for institutions, agencies, and libraries. Please do not send institutional checks for personal subscriptions. Standing orders are accepted.

SINGLE COPIES cost $16.95 when payment accompanies order. (California, New Jersey, New York, and Washington, D.C., residents please include appropriate sales tax.) Billed orders will be charged postage and handling.

DISCOUNTS FOR QUANTITY ORDERS are available. Please write to the address below for information.

ALL ORDERS must include either the name of an individual or an official purchase order number. Please submit your order as follows:
    Subscriptions: specify series and year subscription is to begin
    Single copies: include individual title code (such as ACE 59)

MAIL ALL ORDERS TO:
    Jossey-Bass Publishers
    350 Sansome Street
    San Francisco, California 94104-1342

FOR SUBSCRIPTION SALES OUTSIDE OF THE UNITED STATES, contact any international subscription agency or Jossey-Bass directly.

OTHER TITLES AVAILABLE IN THE
NEW DIRECTIONS FOR ADULT AND CONTINUING EDUCATION SERIES
Ralph G. Brockett, Editor-in-Chief
Alan B. Knox, Consulting Editor